THE U-BOAT WAR

WORLD WAR II FROM PRIMARY SOURCES

BY BOB CARRUTHERS

© Coda Books Ltd
ISBN: 978-1-906783-40-2

CONTENTS

THE U-BOAT WAR

For the brave men who manned the U-Boat fleet the uneven struggle played out between 1939 and 1945 was a real tragedy of catastrophic proportions. In 1939 at the very outset of the war it was already clear to Karl Dönitz that the U-boat mission was futile. As weapon systems, the Type II and Type VII U-boats of 1939 were already inadequate for the task ahead and there were simply not enough of them. To make matters worse, their torpedoes were faulty and their enemies were infinitely superior in every material respect. In their capacity for raw courage and endurance the men of the U-boat fleet demonstrated their determination and dedication to duty.

However, despite some justifiable anxiety, the men of the British Royal Navy and their allies were never close to being outmatched by the U-boats and proved themselves equally tough, resolute and, when occasion demanded, they too would prove totally ruthless.

In December 1941 when Hitler made his typically misguided decision to declare war on the USA the balance tipped even further away from the U-boat fleet. The immense resources of the US Navy and air force secured the prospect of victory. As new aircraft types came into service and Iceland was opened up to allied aircraft the "air gap", the unprotected patch of the mid Atlantic, grew ever smaller. In 1944 the air gap was closed altogether but by then Dönitz had finally accepted defeat in the North Atlantic and ordered his U-boats to withdraw.

A willingness to make the supreme sacrifice in the face of insurmountable odds can be viewed as a noble quality, but it is still futile nonetheless. Blood will never overcome steel and the slender

Grossadmiral Karl Dönitz. Oberbefehlshaber der Kriegsmarine Dönitz was the commander of the U-boat fleet from 1936 until 1945. In 1943 he was appointed to command of the Kreigsmarine as successor to Grossadmiral Erich Raeder. Following Hitler's suicide on 30th April 1945 under the terms of his last testament, Hitler nominated Dönitz to succeeded Hitler as Head Of State (Staatsoberhaupt) and also Supreme Commander of the Armed Forces.

resources of the U-boat fleet were insufficient to bring about the strategic victory which they strived to produce. Despite all of the odds ranged against them, the U-boats did, for a brief time, succeed in wreaking tremendous havoc among allied shipping, and during its short ascendancy the U-boat fleet gave Churchill one of his most genuine and serious bouts of concern for Britain's continued survival. So serious were Churchill's concerns that he later confessed that the Battle of the Atlantic was "the only thing that ever frightened me."

The obvious dangers of serving in the U-boat fleet combined with the highly persuasive activities of the Nazi propaganda machine put a strong gloss on the U-boat war which lionised the achievements of men like Gunter Prein, Joachim Schepke and Otto Kretschmer, but it was a telling statistic that by 1941 two of these heroes were dead and the third was in allied captivity.

It is notoriously difficult to measure the effectiveness of the U-boat campaign. There is no question that the U-boat activities proved massively destructive. Obviously a great deal of vital war equipment and supplies were denied to the allies, but the allied ship yards, particularly after America entered the war proved themselves capable of replenishing the losses and eventually the tonnage launched far outstripped the rate of loss, and despite all of the endeavours to the contrary the allied mercantile fleets actually grew in size as the war progressed.

There was clearly a massive material loss and a damaging effect on allied morale the reverberations of which, as we have seen, reached as far as Churchill himself. However, the actual statistics are difficult to asses with certainty and it is impossible to come up with an overall measure of success or failure's - boats were involved in mine laying exercises as well as direct attacks on allied ships. What is known is that altogether nine U-boats were lost in the first five months of war in 1939 and the sinking of 122 merchant ships was directly attributed to U-boat action. In 1939, the first calendar year of the war, for every U-boat lost, some thirteen allied ships were being sent to the bottom.

Twenty-four U-boats were lost during 1940 against a loss of 471 allied ships, the loss of which were attributed to U-boat action. This was to prove to be the high point of the U-boats with almost twenty allied ships sunk in exchange for each U-boat which was lost.

In 1941, the turning point of the war in the Atlantic was already in sight. The rate of U-boat losses continued to climb with 35 boats sunk for a reduced annual tally of 432 ships sunk by U-boat action. An exchange rate of just over twelve allied ships sunk for each U-boat sunk. A lower rate than had been achieved in the first year of the war and a sharp decline on 1940.

During 1942, the rate of U-boat destruction rose sharply as 86 boats were sunk in return for 1159 allied ships. This was approaching the level of destruction which, if maintained, could actually threaten the lifeline to the UK and it was this dark hour which gave Churchill serious grounds for concern. Despite all the extra resources deployed by The Kriegsmarine however, the rate of ships sunk by each boat lost steadfastly hovered around thirteen.

By 1943, the Enigma breakthrough was having its effect. Convoy tactics had improved, air cover and radar had improved dramatically and in consequence the number of U-boats sunk climbed to a catastrophic 242 boats. Only 463 allied ships had been sunk in return. The exchange rate had fallen from thirteen allied ships sunk for every U-boat lost in 1942 to just under two allied ships sunk for each U-boat lost in 1943. The allies could make good their losses but with the fortunes of war running against Germany on every front, the evidence was now plain to see - the U-boat cause was hopeless. The rapidly mounting losses and other important factors such as the constantly shifting balance of technology in favour of the allies, who were gaining in firepower, resources and tonnage of shipping launched, all conspired to render the decision to carry on the battle

The relatively small bulk of the U-boats allowed the entire craft to be dragged on to dry land for the frequent bouts of essential maintenance.

beyond 1943 criminally suicidal.

With the Enigma code now cracked and the allies in receipt of detailed operational information the consequences were likely to be calamitous. Dönitz remained blissfully unaware of the Enigma developments but it was clear that the battle for the Atlantic convoy routes had been lost and Dönitz ordered his boats to withdraw from the North Atlantic. Elsewhere he was forced to continue the uneven fight. The result was disastrous for the brave men of The Kriegsmarine. 250 U-boats were sunk in 1944, which unsurprisingly was the worst year of the war so far for U-boat losses. In return for this alarming rate of loss, the Grey Wolves sank just 132 ships which meant that almost two U-boats were now being lost for each allied ship sunk.

The advent of airborne radar and advanced submarine detection devices should have signalled the end of the fight. By 1944, the U-boat war had clearly been lost and despite the desperate search for effective counter measures and improved U-boat designs there was simply no way back. Still there was to be no respite for the U-boats. 1945 was even worse with 120 boats destroyed in action for the loss of just 56 allied ships during the first few months of the year before the final peace arrived early in May 1945. By the end of the war over two U-boats were being sunk for each allied ship which was sent to the bottom.

All together 731 U-boats were lost in combat between 1939 and

1945. A further 200 were scuttled as part of Operation Regenbogen in May 1945. This massive sacrifice of men and resources represented the equivalent resource needed to field some 12,000 to 15,000 battle tanks, a resource which could have made a real impact on the land war. It is important to note that other methods for attacking allied shipping in the form of mines laid by surface vessels, surface raiders and aircraft attacks were equally successful and only just over 50% of allied shipping losses were attributed to U-boats. Of 5219 allied ships lost during the course of the war with Germany only 2827 were attributed to U-boat action.

In many respects this was a war that should never have been fought. In 1938, a series of war games and manoeuvres carried out by the Kreigsmarine had conclusively proven that the effective blockade of the British Isles would require an active force of 300 U-Boats operating in the Atlantic. This figure was based on a loss rate to the U-boat force of 50%. When actual combat losses, boats in transit, boats under repair, training and construction were taken into consideration it was clear that in practice the U-boat force would have needed something like one thousand operational vessels to stand even the remotest prospect of success. The reality was that when war was declared the U-boat fleet amounted to just eleven training ships and 46 combat vessels. Of the combat craft, twenty were the small costal Type II boats and two were the unsuccessful Type I design, leaving a total force of just 24 ocean going U-boats ready for combat.

To begin the battle for the North Atlantic in 1939 with just 24 suitable combat ready boats was a futile mission. Although many more were under construction and the build programme was being hastily accelerated, the nine U-boats lost to enemy action in 1939 was proportionately a very heavy cross to bear and heralded the nightmare to come. The vanishingly slight chances of success for the U-boats in the beginning declined ever more rapidly as anti-submarine measures grew more efficient and deadly. There were simply never enough U-Boats to achieve the strategic objective of choking the British Isles and the high command of the Kreigsmarine knew this to be the case. As the war progressed, the addition of extra operational theatres in the South Atlantic, Arctic, Caribbean, Mediterranean and Far East stretched those thin resources beyond the point where even the faintest hope of strategic success remained.

On land the Wermacht achieved some strategic successes, but after 1942 these were in short supply. In retrospect one of the main values of the U-boat fleet was to bolster a propaganda effort which gave false hope to the hard pressed German people. The exploits of the U-boats made a great story for cinema news reels, propaganda magazines and newspapers. The sea wolves were glamourised and hero worshipped. In order to feed the relentless appetite for success stories many U-boats were accompanied by film and photo journalists from the PK propaganda companies (Propaganda Kompanie), one of whom was Lothar–Gunther Buchheim, famous as the author of 'Das Boot', the fictionalised account of a journey which the writer as a PK member had undertaken in U96.

Over the six years of World War Two over 1200 U-boats were actually commissioned into the Kreigsmarine. Of these 731 were lost in combat and the inescapable fact is that never at any time did the losses they inflicted equate to the rate at which new allied ships were being built. The pressures of the uneven struggle grew worse as the war progressed. A U-boat was a complex vessel to sail which needed experienced handling, but as experienced crews were lost in the remorseless jaws of combat, less and less experienced crews were being sent to sea. From mid 1943 these boats were frequently being lost on their very first mission without ever having had the chance to strike a blow and a disconcertingly high number appear to have been lost to crew error. Some 52 U-boats are recorded as missing in action. Inevitably a number of these boats will have been lost to enemy action or mechanical failure but a substantial number are thought to lie on the bottom of the ocean as a result of inexperienced crews making fatal errors in the handling of these unforgiving craft.

Happy faces as a U-boat returns safely to port following a successful mission. This image from the pages of Die Wehrmacht was a common enough scene in 1939 and 1940, but grew increasingly rare as the war progressed and the grim reality of an unsuccessful campaign took its toll on the U-boat fleet.

Contemporary reporting on the U-boat war from the pages of Die Wehrmacht in 1940. The picture sequence on the left shows the successful torpedoing of an allied freighter by a U-boat operating on the surface and the crew receiving decorations from Dönitz on arrival in port.

The photographic account of a successful U-boat patrol as reported in the pages of Die Wehrmacht in 1940.

During the early stages of the war Signal Magazine was able to boast that the allied bomber campaign was not hindering the construction and operation of the U-boats. The situation would change dramatically over the course of the war.

Trotzdem...! Unbehindert von anglo-amerikanischen Bomben geht die Arbeit auf deutschen Werften im europäischen Raum weiter. PK-Aufnahme

THE U-BOATS

Although they are frequently referred to as submarines, the U-boats of World War Two were not true submarines. They were essentially diesel powered surface ships which could travel submerged for short periods and at slow speed using electric power from their auxiliary engines. They were more properly described by the term submersibles. The Achilles heel of the U-boat fleet in the early part of the war was the fact that the boat had to surface in order to recharge the electric cells which propelled the submerged craft. Later in the war the Schnorchel device was introduced. This device was based on captured Dutch technology and is often referred to by its Dutch name the "Snorkel", which allowed the submerged U-boat to draw oxygen from the surface and thus travel submerged on diesel engines. This simple expedient massively extended the range of the submerged craft, but could only be used in relatively calm seas.

The U-boat fleet was the subject of constant research and frenzied development. By 1945 some revolutionary designs were ready to enter service but the U-boat war was sustained by three main types of craft and each had glaring limitations.

TYPE II BOATS

The first Type to see service was the small costal U-boat known as the Type II, initially built by the Deutche Werke in Kiel. As events progressed, the Type II appeared in four variants labelled from A-D, each successive variant offering advances in armament and capability. Weighing in at only three hundred and eighty tons, the Type II initially had a surface cruising range of just 1600 nautical miles at eight knots. Submerged, the boats could travel for just thirty five nautical miles at a maximum speed of just four knots. The boats had a good diving range and could safely descend to 150 metres. Fifty of these small vessels known to their crews as "canoes" or "ducks" were commissioned between 1935 and 1941 when production ceased. The first variants of this small vessel were crewed by just twenty five men and carried only five torpedoes (known colloquially to the crew as "aale", the German for eels). The Type II was not limited to a direct attack role and could also carry twelve mines when the craft were deployed for mine laying duties. Crucially this type carried no deck gun so the ability to attack shipping on the surface was lost. As the first boats to be built following the abandonment of the Versailles treaty, these were the training ground for the new U-boat arm. Tactically their use was limited to short range costal missions and these vessels had no part to play in the struggle for the wide Atlantic.

A PK (Propaganda Company) at work recording the formal welcome of a victorious U-boat on its return to its home port.

TYPE VII BOATS

The main U-boat type which contested the war in the Atlantic was the medium Type VII. Over six hundred of this class were eventually commissioned. This design was larger and faster than the Type II and the first variants carried eleven torpedoes and, more importantly, mounted the highly effective 88mm deck gun which allowed these craft to engage allied shipping on the surface. The Type VIIA also had a much more practical range of 6200 nautical miles at ten knots and could travel 94 miles submerged at the very slow speed of four knots. At a pinch the Type VII could also dive to a depth of 220 metres. The Type VIIB improved on the range of the early variants by a further 2500 miles which was produced by the addition of the characteristic saddle tanks which held thirty tons of fuel and gave the U-boats their distinctive shape. Three additional torpedoes could be crammed into the hull of the Type VIIB giving a total complement of fourteen.

These much loved boats carried a crew of between 42 and 46. The Type VIIB was the variant which was commanded by the most

The process of training the fledging U-boat fleet continued at Gotenhaven.

famous captains of the early war such as Prien, Schepke and Kretschmer. U-48 initially commanded by Kretschmer was in fact the most successful U-boat of the war. A survivor of twelve operational patrols she sank 51 allied ships before being retired as a training vessel in 1943. Some 23 examples of the Type VIIB boats were commissioned and built from 1938 onwards. The Type IIB was built with only a single rudder and was less manoeuvrable than it's replacement, the Type VIIC. 568 further boats of the improved Type VIIC were subsequently commissioned. First entering service in 1940, this type was to prove the work horse of the U-Boat fleet. Powered by two powerful and highly reliable six cylinder diesel engines chiefly built by the MAN company, these all important engines were affectionately known as "jumbos" to the crewmen. The Type VIIC was built from 1938 to 1944 and remained in service until the bitter end. Six examples of a larger mine laying variant, the Type VIID, were also introduced into service from 1942 onwards, but these proved unsuccessful and five of the six boats were lost with all hands. The Type VIIC could make an impressive twelve to fifteen knots on the surface but her Achilles heel still lay with the fact that the boat could only travel the relatively short distance of 95 nautical miles when submerged.

On surfacing the electric motors required to be recharged by the

Early type VII boats commissioned from 1935 onwards.

Diesel engines. This was done by switching the clutch of one of the "jumbos" to recharge the electric engines while the other at full strain drove the U-boat forward through the waves. The recharging process took a full eight hours and during that time the U-boat was highly vulnerable to surface or air attack. It was possible to engage both the jumbos to recharge the electric motors which reduced the time taken to just four hours, but during that time the U-boat had to remain motionless on the surface. The later introduction of the snorchel device helped the situation as the device drew air in from the surface and allowed the U-boats to travel submerged on diesel power. The depth at which a U-boat could travel submerged using the snorchel was obviously limited to the length of the air intake. In order to prevent water from being drawn into the engines a valve switched off the intake if the intake was swamped. Rough seas made the device all but unusable.

THE TYPE IX

The largest of the three main types of operational U-boat was the Type IX ocean going vessel which could carry up to 22 torpedoes, packed a heavier 105mm deck gun and, with the introduction of the IXB, this class of vessel had a vastly improved range of 15000 nautical miles. Altogether some 193 examples of the Type IX were commissioned and built. On average the 14 Type IXB boats proved to be the most effective design of the war sinking on average 100,000 tons per boat commissioned, although the statistic is somewhat skewed by the fact that on one spectacular cruise Hessler's U-107 sank almost 100,000 tons of allied shipping off Freetown in West Africa.

From 1942 a number of Type IX vessels were converted into the supply role. These were the Milchkuh or "Milk Cows" specially adapted to resupply the fleet at sea and thus extend U-boat operations by Type VII boats to include the Caribbean and eastern seaboard of North America. This force multiplier class was a weak link and was targeted and hunted to extinction by the allies. Some 289 crewmen representing over 60% of the crews who served in the small fleet of Milchkuhs died in action.

THE FORMATION OF THE FLEET

The terms of the Treaty of Versailles, signed in 1919, forbade Germany the right to posses a U-boat fleet. In 1917 the German U-boat fleet of World War One had come very close to achieving its strategic objective of cutting off all supply to the British Isles by means of an effective blockade. Following the introduction of counter measures such as those pioneered by the Anti-Submarine detection Committee, anti-submarine methods had definitely improved during 1918, but as the war ended the balance of power still lay with the U-boats. The British in particular were therefore adamant that Germany should be completely forbidden the right to possess submarines or to develop submarines in future. The Reichsmarine of the inter-war years was intended to be a small force dedicated solely to the defence of the German Fatherland.

This was a very wise precaution on the part of those who sought to preserve the peace, but it was an anathema to the German armed forces who from as early as 1922 were engaged in clandestine work to re-establish a U-boat fleet. This unwholesome situation reached crisis levels soon after Adolf Hitler came to power in 1933. Hitler's Fascist agenda was built on the primitive creed of the survival of the fittest. His policies were expansionist, nationalistic and above all militarist. These were exactly the kind of ambitions which the Versailles Treaty had been designed to prevent. In practice, little was done to enforce the terms of the treaty and the very reason for it's existence was undermined by a policy of appeasement and led to a series of disastrous decisions by both civilian and military leaders culminating in the naïve Munich Agreement of 29th September 1938 and the famously misplaced declaration by Neville Chamberlain that we should all have "peace in our time".

As early as 1935 however, Hitler had grown in confidence and on 16th March the crucial provisions of the Versailles Treaty were formally rescinded with the announcement that Germany would re-arm. Germany's remarkably advanced ability to re-arm was not all Hitler's doing. Prior to 1935 Germany had embarked upon a course of clandestine military experimentation which had seen the parallel development of the tanks, aircraft, ships, submarines and artillery which equipped the Wermacht in World War Two. These activities predated even the rise of Hitler and ironically, given what would happen later, much of the clandestine tank development programme had taken place deep inside Soviet Russia.

It would not have been wise to place all of Germany's developing military secrets in the Soviet basket; the secret submarine development programme was therefore undertaken in conjunction with Finland and Spain, two sympathetic maritime nations. As early as 1922 Admiral Paul Behnke, Commander-in-Chief of the small post war Reichsmarine had secretly authorised the covert operations which would result in the creation of a new generation of U-boats. The initial design work was undertaken by a coterie of engineers seconded from the Krupp company. As the designs were completed the manufacturing process was undertaken locally by Ingeniurskantoor voor Scheepsbouw, a Dutch registered company controlled from Germany. The foreign manufacturing stage was undertaken in conjunction with the tacit support of the pro-German, Spanish and Finnish governments. The Ingeniurskantoor voor Scheepsbouw company also found a genuine order for two U-boats which were to be built in Turkey for the Turkish navy. Although Turkish ship yards and ship builders were engaged, the project was very much under the control of Ingeniurskantoor voor Scheepsbouw and the precious ship building knowledge was retained by Germany.

Rohde and his comrades take the oath in Breda, Holland.

The order for the two Turkish U-boats also brought with it the welcome requirement for an accompanying training school. It was obviously necessary to establish a school for the training of the Turkish submariners who were to crew the submarines, but seizing the opportunity, the activities of the school was soon expanded to include German crews. At this stage Germany was still paying lip service to the Versailles Treaty and these crews initially were formed from retired naval personnel only. In 1933, U-boat training finally started in earnest in Germany itself with the establishment of The Unterseebootsabwerschule at Kiel. Although the title of the school translated as Anti-submarine warfare, the reality was that the establishment was entirely dedicated to training U-boat crews.

The first concrete result of the international subterfuge by Germany and her accomplices was the launch of a small 25 man submarine built by the Fins under German supervision. She was the first of three costal U-boats built in Finland under the clandestine U-boat building programme. More importantly she was the prototype of the Type II costal "canoe" which was to be the training ground for the nascent U-boat fleet. In 1936 the Finnish government exercised its option to purchase the vessel and she became the Finnish submarine Vesikko and served throughout World War Two, surviving to become a ship museum. She still stands there today as an exhibit on the Finnish island of Suomenlinna. The three Vesikko class submarines constructed in Finland were followed by a further three medium submarines designated as Vetehinens, the forerunners of the highly successful medium Type VII. In Spain a single large ocean submarine, the E1, was also produced. There were endless complications with this design. Even the launch was a fiasco as the boat immediately ran aground, but it was the first in a tortuous development line which would eventually lead to the Type IX ocean going submarine.

Begegnung mit Schiffbrüchigen

U-BOOTE HELFEN DEM FEIND

Unsere Kriegsmarine bekämpft den Feind, wo sie ihn trifft. Vom höchsten Norden bis zum tropischen Süden kreuzen unsere Kriegsschiffe, gefährliche Gegner für die feindliche Schiffahrt. Aber der deutsche Soldat kämpft ritterlich, auch auf den Meeren. Wir haben es erlebt — wir denken an den Fall „Altmark" —, daß englische Soldaten auf hilflose oder wehrlose Deutsche schossen. Unsere Seeleute helfen dem besiegten Gegner. Es ist einem U-Boot natürlich nicht möglich, Schiffbrüchige

an Bord zu nehmen oder Rettungsboote weite Strecken über See zu schleppen. Aber jeder Schiffbrüchige wird, selbst unter schwierigsten Verhältnissen, mit nötigstem Proviant und Trinkwasser versehen, auf den richtigen Kurs gebracht. Er ist kein Feind mehr, sondern ein Mensch, dem geholfen werden muß, soweit es die Lage nur immer erlaubt. Unsere Bilder berichten von der Hilfe, die von einem U-Boot nach der Versenkung feindlicher bewaffneter Dampfer den Schiffbrüchigen geleistet wird

Mitten im Atlantik hat ein U-Boot ein treibendes Rettungsfloß gesichtet, auf dem sich drei Schiffbrüchige befinden. Durch Winkspruch wird den dreien mitgeteilt, daß das U-Boot längsseits kommen wird

Es ist unmöglich, die Schiffbrüchigen an Bord zu nehmen, aber da sich das Floß auf einer der meistbefahrenen Schiffsrouten befinden und die See völlig ruhig ist, kann damit gerechnet werden, daß die Schiffbrüchigen, die mit Trinkwasser, Brot und Konserven versehen worden sind, bald weiteres Hilfe finden. Mit einem Handedruck verabschieden sie sich von der hilfbereiten Besatzung des U-Bootes

... das Boot kommt längsseits; die Besatzung, ohne Unterschied, ob schwarz oder weiß, wird vorübergehend an Deck genommen, damit die Mannschaft ihr Boot ausrichten und für die Fortsetzung der Fahrt mit deutscher Hilfe wieder seetüchtig machen kann

... ein schwarzer Ruß- und Ölfleck zeigt die Stelle, wo soeben ein feindlicher Dampfer versenkt wurde. Eine der Rettungsumgeschlagen und treibt mit 12 Mann Besatzung kieloben. Englische Kapitäne haben es fertig gebracht, deutsche Schiffin gleicher Lage zu beschießen. Aber deutsche Seeleute kämpfen ritterlich und helfen dem besiegten Gegner ...

PK-Aufnahmen: Kriegsberichter Dietrich (H.H.) 4

A German propaganda account of the fair treatment of wrecked Allied crew men. Dönitz expressly prohibited actions such as these and at Nurnberg he was subsequently accused, and found guilty, of waging unrestricted submarine warfare as a result of U-boats following his War Order No. 154 in 1939, and another similar order issued after the Laconia incident in 1942. Under the terms of these orders U-boat captains were ordered not to rescue survivors from ships attacked by submarine. By issuing these two orders Donitz acted contrary to the Naval Protocol of 1936 to which Germany acceded, and which reaffirmed the rules of submarine warfare laid down in the London Naval Agreement of 1930. As a result he was found guilty of causing Germany to be in breach of the Second London Naval Treaty of 1936 and was sentenced to ten years which he served in Spandau Prison in West Berlin.

These pages from the propaganda magazine Signal accurately document the fact that the U-boat campaign had reached the coast of North America and the Caribbean was posing a serious threat to merchant shipping on the eastern Atlantic seaboard.

VOR DEN TOREN NEW YORKS

Für die Vereinigten Staaten hat der Krieg mit einigen Überraschungen begonnen. Als man in Washington den Schock des japanischen Angriffs auf Pearl Harbour noch nicht überwunden hatte, sah man sich plötzlich deutschen U-Booten gegenüber, die in den Gewässern vor der nordamerikanischen und kanadischen Küste die amerikanische Schiffahrt in unerwartet erfolgreichem Maße unsicher machten. In wenigen Tagen der letzten Januarwoche versenkten deutsche U-Boote sozusagen vor den Augen der Amerikaner über 40 Schiffe mit mehr als 300 000 BRT. Drei Tanker wurden unmittelbar vor dem Hafen von New York versenkt. — Die „Schlacht im Atlantik" geht also weiter, und die deutschen Seestreitkräfte erzielen trotz der schwierigen Wetterlage außerordentliche Erfolge selbst in Gewässern, die so weit von ihren Stützpunkten entfernt sind wie die Gewässer der Vereinigten Staaten und Kanadas. Wie sich ein Angriff auf einen Geleitzug durch Unterseeboote vollzieht, zeigen wir auf diesen Seiten zum ersten Male in einer genauen, auf die Uhrzeit abgestimmten Zeichnung.

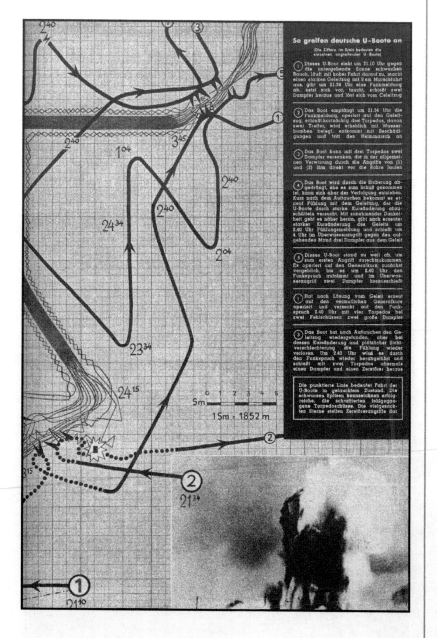

So greifen deutsche U-Boote an

(Die Ziffern im Kreis bedeuten die einzelnen angreifenden U-Boote)

① Dieses U-Boot sieht um 21.10 Uhr gegen die untergehende Sonne schwachen Rauch, läuft mit hoher Fahrt darauf zu, macht einen starken Geleitzug mit 9 sm Marschfahrt aus, gibt um 21.36 Uhr eine Funkmeldung ab, setzt sich vor, taucht, schießt zwei Dampfer heraus und löst sich vom Geleitzug

② Das Boot empfängt um 21.34 Uhr die Funkmeldung, operiert auf den Geleitzug, schießt hartnäckig drei Torpedos, davon zwei Treffer, wird erheblich mit Wasserbomben belegt, entkommt mit Beschädigungen und tritt den Heimmarsch an

③ Das Boot kann mit drei Torpedos zwei Dampfer versenken, die in der allgemeinen Verwirrung durch die Angriffe von ① und ② ihm direkt vor die Rohre laufen

④ Das Boot wird durch die Sicherung abgedrängt, ehe es zum Schuß gekommen ist, kann sich aber der Verfolgung entziehen. Kurs nach dem Auftauchen bekommt es erneut Fühlung mit dem Geleitzug, der die U-Boote durch starke Kursänderung abzuschütteln versucht. Mit zunehmender Dunkelheit geht es näher heran, gibt nach erneuter starker Kursänderung des Geleits um 2.40 Uhr Fühlungsmeldung und schießt um 4 Uhr im Überwasserangriff gegen den aufgehenden Mond drei Dampfer aus dem Geleit

⑤ Dieses U-Boot stand zu weit ab, um zum ersten Angriff zurechtzukommen. Es operiert auf den Generalkurs, zunächst vergeblich, bis es um 2.40 Uhr den Funkspruch aufnimmt und im Überwasserangriff zwei Dampfer herausschießt

⑥ Hat nach Lösung vom Geleit erneut auf den vermutlichen Generalkurs operiert und versenkt auf den Funkspruch 2.40 Uhr mit vier Torpedos bei zwei Fehlschüssen zwei große Dampfer

⑦ Das Boot hat nach Auftauchen den Geleitzug wiedergefunden, aber bei dessen Kursänderung und plötzlicher Sichtverschlechterung die Fühlung wieder verloren. Um 2.40 Uhr wird es durch den Funkspruch wieder herangeführt und schießt mit zwei Torpedos abermals einen Dampfer und einen Zerstörer heraus

Die punktierte Linie bedeutet Fahrt der U-Boote in getauchtem Zustand. Die schwarzen Spitzen kennzeichnen erfolgreiche, die schraffierten fehlgegangene Torpedoschüsse. Die vielzackten Sterne stellen Zerstörerangriffe dar

0 1 2 3 4 5

5m

1 Sm = 1852 m

The emergence of the Wolf Pack tactic is demonstrated quite openly in this article which allegedly records the fate of an Allied Gelietzug (convoy) successfully challenged by the U-boats. The propaganda magazine states for anyone who will listen that, despite its Zerstörer Sicherung (Defensive screen of destroyers), the convoy has suffered heavy losses.

All of this huge effort could easily have been in vain. In the early Thirties there had been serious international talks aimed at outlawing the submarine as a form of warfare which was universally acknowledged as "barbaric", but this broad consensus was never ratified in treaty form. By 1935 the opportunity had gone. Hitler openly renounced the Versailles Treaty and Britain cravenly accepted Hitler's abandonment and meekly agreed that Hitler could reintroduce the U-boat into The Kriegsmarine - provided that the overall size of the German fleet was limited to a size no larger than 35% of the massive British fleet.

Amazingly under the terms of a Naval agreement dated 18th June 1935, the British agreed that Germany could own a submarine fleet 45% of the size of the British equivalent. No one seems to have seriously considered the fact that the Royal Navy had a global responsibility, policing an Empire on which the sun never set. Only 30% of the British fleet was likely to be in home waters at any time so Hitler was in effect being granted local superiority. Unbelievably the treaty allowed the Germans to expand their U-boat fleet to parity with the Royal Navy with the simple requirement that due

A Begleitschipp used for training and supply alongside a flotilla of Type II boats.

notification was given in advance. This was just one more in a series of shocking blunders which gave Hitler confidence and ensured the initial successes of the Wermacht in World War Two.

U1, commanded by Kluas Werth, was the first of the six Type II costal U-boats built during 1935 by the Deutsche Werke at Kiel. The work had actually begun under conditions of secrecy in 1933 but the launch of the vessel in 1935 was a public act of defiance, Germany was officially on the march once more.

Numbered from U1 through to U6 these small vessels were organised into the first U-boat training flotilla, the Unterseebootschulflottille. The school was highly effective and as the first of the medium Type VIIA boats, numbered U27 through to U36, began to roll off the slipways, trained crews could be provided from the Unterseebootschulflottille.

Later in 1935 the bones of the first operational U-boat flotilla, "Weddigen", was established under Kapitan zur See Karl Dönitz as the first of the Type VII's became ready for commissioning in September 1935. Dönitz was an experienced U-boat veteran of World War I and had practical experience of command of a vessel at sea to draw upon. Having spent the intervening 20 years studying the lessons of the first war and developing new theories on submarine warfare, Dönitz was the obvious choice to head up the rapidly expanding U-boat fleet. In 1936 he was confirmed as Führer der Unterseeboote. Dönitz served throughout the war as head of the

The "Jumbos" were the two huge diesel engines which provided sea going power and charged the power cells which drove the electric engines.

U-boat arm and later as head of the Kriegsmarine. He was meticulous and incredibly thorough, debriefing many of his captains personally after each mission, rewarding success and ruthlessly punishing failure. Dönitz loved the crews and even allowed favoured captains to address him by the German personal "du". The down side to Dönitz as a commander was his willingness to conform to the wishes of Adolf Hitler. Dönitz did not have the capacity for arguing with the Fuerher which marked the stormy relations between Hitler and the likes of Raeder, Rommel or Guderian. Unlike many of his colleagues, Dönitz was a committed Nazi and he fell under the Furher's mesmeric spell. In his relationship with Hitler, Dönitz was much more akin to sycophants such as Jodel or Keitel and as a result his U-boat crews paid a heavy price for their commander's failure to intervene more effectively on their behalf. Donitz was an able strategist and he did have the political skills which saw the U-boat fleet withdrawn from the North Atlantic albeit after the damage had been done.

Although the U-boat fleet was failing quite spectacularly in its strategic task, the scale of the defeat was much less obvious than the disasters in Russia or Normandy. On land a military reverse was all too obvious and could not be concealed. The progress of the U-boat war was much more opaque but it was defeat nonetheless. Dönitz however was never to experience the full wrath of Hitler. Commanders who failed on land would inevitably find accusations of treachery heaped upon the usual outpouring of bile which descended upon the victims of the Feurher's temper. For this reason Dönitz survived the whole war and was named as Hitler's successor following the Fuerher's cowardly suicide.

One unforgivable aspect of Dönitz behaviour was his failure to plan for the introduction of a successor to Enigma. It is a vital tenant of encryption that codes are scrapped and replaced. By allowing the system to evolve Dönitz was partly responsible for one of the biggest blunders of the war.

"IN MY BOAT, NO ONE SHOUTED 'HOORAY!' IT WAS MORE LIKE, 'OH, GOD, THE POOR DEVILS!'"
HERBERT LANGE

U-BOAT TRAINING AND SELECTION

Checking levels of fuel oil was one of the thousands of tasks which had to be completed every day in order to ensure the smooth running of the U-boat.

U-boat warfare has all the hallmarks of guerrilla fighting. It is furtive and clandestine. It relies on the silent, stealthy approach, the ambush and the fast escape before the enemy can respond. Surprise is its natural currency. Between 1939 and 1945, it took exceptional men with exceptional nerve to fight this kind of war, and do it in an enclosed, claustrophobic atmosphere from the unnatural confines of the world beneath the sea.

The German surface raiders - Scharnhorst, Gneisenau, Admiral Hipper, the pocket battleship Admiral Graf Spee - received most of the publicity in the Second World War at sea. They acquired a glamorous reputation for daring, even in Britain. The Royal Navy's pursuit of Graf Spee, which was scuttled by her captain, Hans Langsdorff, outside Montevideo harbour on 17 December 1939 as the British task force waited for her outside, was predictably characterised by Goebbels propaganda ministry as Greek tragedy in which a noble adversary was driven to death by an unkind fate. Despite their headline-making successes, the activities of the German surface ships were curtailed by the overwhelming strength of the Royal Navy and they had only a minor influence on the conduct, and outcome, of the war in the Atlantic. The U-boats became the defacto backbone of the offensive war.

At the start of the War, the U-boats were relatively few - only fifty-seven boats in all, a fraction of the huge fleet Hitler had promised the commander of the Kriegsmarine's submarine arm. Even so, their importance was fully realised and so was the special nature of submarine warfare. Great care was taken to ensure that crews were an elite. Physical fitness requirements for men serving on the U-boats were much more stringent than they were for other combatants. Ernst Gunther Rohde was one of the few who passed the test.

'If you were physically healthy, then you could join the Navy, but for the U-boats, they were a special breed who underwent a special medical examination to ensure that they were what was called 'fit for U-boats'. When I volunteered at the end of 1940, they first of all put me through the mangle as we called it, in every aspect of my health and I was pronounced "fit for U-boats".'

Physical fitness alone was not enough even after the stringent medical checks, the numbers who actually served on the U-boats could be whittled down further, as Herbert Lange remembers:

'There were twenty of us who were selected as being fit to serve in the U-boats and we had to go straight to Wilhelmshaven for a medical inspection. After that, only eight men were left, eight men who satisfied the health and fitness regulations. I was one of them. We were all proud of that, I have to say.'

U-boat crews went through intensive training before putting to sea.

Ernst Rhode recalls the daily routine of the Officer Training course with the 24 Unterseebootsflottille at Memel, which was hard going indeed.

'When I was with the training commando in Memel, we went out every day with four torpedoes in the tubes and four in reserve which we used as replacements. There was a target ship, the Daressalam which sailed around in a square and sometimes a boat would suddenly appear. You had to fire at this angle or at that angle, and the torpedoes ran ten or eleven metres below the surface and ran underneath the ship. We had acoustic equipment on board and in the head of the torpedo, where the dynamite is normally packed, there was a large searchlight and when it ran below the ship we could see exactly if it had run towards the bow, amidships or astern. They went for three or four kilometres to where there were torpedo recovery ships.'

It was now that the process of salvaging the precious torpoedoes began, another hard manual task as Herbert Lange recalls.

Ernst Rohde, an 18 year old U-Boat volunteer. 'U-Boat crews were a special breed - you had to be 'fit' for the U-Boats'

Survivors of the torpedoed US ship the Atlantis were taken aboard U126. This highly dangerous practice was later prohibited by Dönitz.

'Once the pressurised air had escaped from the torpedoes, then, because the head had such a large volume, it stood upright in the water. At the front, there was carbide which gave off smoke and smelled horrible when it came in contact with the water. The torpedo recovery ship was able to see clearly where the torpedo was, bobbing around in the water, because it was only 55cm in diameter and just about six meters long and moved with the currents. They were recovered, and prepared for reuse on the recovery ships. At the base in Memel, they were handed over to a tender where they were refilled with pressurised air. That happened each day over the whole week and two or three times during the night when we had to practise night firing, that had to be practised at night. We could only fire if the wind was no stronger than force five, the boats could have withstood more, but a torpedo weighed perhaps 2,000 kilos, 2-3,000 kilos and we couldn't cope with a wind stronger than force five. We did that every day and for the crew it was unpleasant. Normally on the sea, you sailed for half a day under water, but we had to surface each time we had fired and then on alarm we had to dive again.'

WAR IS DECLARED

For Herbert Lange the day was not far off when all this practice was going to be put to use in a real battle. By 1939 Herbert had qualified from 24 Unterseebootsflottille and was already on board the U28, out in the Atlantic, west of Ireland, when war was declared on 3 September 1939:

'I remember the radio message coming through, 'Hostilities against England have been opened'. We didn't shout 'hooray'; we said, 'Hm!'. If that's the way it has to be, we told ourselves, then, roll up your sleeves and get on with it. We weren't actually pleased about it. We knew that our adversary, England, was a hard adversary. No, we weren't that enthusiastic. We had all volunteered, the U-Boats were somehow something special. But we knew it wasn't going to be easy.'

The German U-boat campaign was unlimited warfare from the start and the early strategy was to prowl British waters making daylight attacks from periscope depth. The submarines would concentrate on the slowest and therefore the easiest quarry, and found easy prey attacking lone merchant ships. Most of the destruction of Allied ships took place on the surface at this time. Almost before the crew of a ship knew what was happening, a U-boat would suddenly appear from the depths and let loose with its deck gun.

An attack on the surface was potentially a dangerous manoeuvre. Surfacing meant a U-boat was at risk from destroyers or aircraft that were prowling the area. There was usually no choice, though, because of the limited space on board a U-boat. Surfacing frequently was necessary too, because the electric motors needed regular recharging. Even so, there were benefits and Herbert Lange enjoyed them.

'After some time submerged, we needed air. And during the first

Herbert Lange, who served as an NCO in the German navy throughout the war.

year of the war, we sailed on the surface a lot, so that as far as our health was concerned, it was lovely, breathing in the fresh Atlantic air.'

Surfacing and diving underwater became a regular routine. The U-boats typically surfaced at night to recharge the batteries which drove the electric motors. If only one of the jumbos was clutched for recharging, the boat could move under the power of one engine. If both diesel engines were clutched to recharge the batteries, the U-boat remained stationary for about four hours, usually from 2000 hours to midnight.

When the batteries were fully charged, the U-boat dived below the surface, resurfaced shortly before daybreak to air the boat and then remained submerged for the rest of the day. The first German 'kill' of the War was controversial. On 4th September 1939, U30 sank the Athenia, a British passenger liner, with the loss of 128 lives. Contrary to the London Naval Agreement of 1935, the passengers were not taken off before the vessel was attacked. Britain regarded this as an atrocity, but Goebbels' propaganda machine was already in operation with the counter claim that the British had themselves destroyed the Athenia in order to provide an excuse to get round another clause in the Naval Agreement: in this instance the ban on arming merchant vessels.

According to Werner Ziemer, a vessel carrying armaments, a merchant ship or any other, was easy to identify.

'You could tell if there was war material on board by the amount of weaponry carried on the decks. In the early part of the War, a boarding party would be sent on board and the ship was searched for contraband. If contraband were found, the crew was taken off in boats and the ship was sunk.'

At this early stage, the Germans would supply an enemy crew with provisions and tow them to a safe distance before sinking their ship. If they saw enemy sailors in the water, they would fish them out, take them prisoner and then deposit them on a nearby coast. All this gave the submariners a reputation for chivalry. On the Murmansk run to Russia, for example, the U-boat that torpedoed the American freighter Fairfield City after its crew had abandoned ship, surfaced afterwards to give the sailors directions towards the nearest land. This, though, became an isolated incident late in the War. As Heinz Reiners explains, the honourable, humanitarian way of fighting did not last.

'In the later years of the War, it was no longer possible. I experienced this myself: survivors, men swimming in the water would be machine-gunned.'

Werner Ziemer had first hand experience of the dangers of surface actions.

'The Boarding party was fired at and the hatches on the sides of the ship flew open and then the U-boat itself was fired upon. This was how the war became more and more merciless, more ruthless on both sides.'

Surfacing to pick up survivors brought fresh and to Donitz, unacceptable risks. Eventually Donitz was forced to issue a direct order that the U-boats should not endanger their missions by searching for survivors. This was to lead to his trial and subsequent imprisonment after Nuremberg.

All of this still lay in the future when Herr Ziemer was busy fighting the war at the sharp end. 'Of course, we didn't search a

A cheery group aboard U47 prepare to embark upon another mission.

> "WE CREPT ALONG AND IT WAS A REAL GAME OF CAT AND MOUSE."
> WERNER VOIGTLANDER

33

tanker before we sank it. We knew what it was carrying and we weren't going to let the enemy get hold of it. There were also empty ships sailing back to England across the Atlantic. Tonnage was important. If a ship went to the bottom, it couldn't be loaded up again. So we sank the empty ships whenever we got the chance.'

Warships, of course, were automatic targets for the U-boats. On 17th September, the U29 sank the aircraft carrier HMS Courageous. That was followed in October by an exploit which greatly raised the profile of German submariners. U47, commanded by Gunther Prien, managed to penetrate Scapa Flow by night on 13-14 October 1939 and in the confined waters fired two torpedo salvos which sank the battleship HMS Royal Oak. Although U47 was operating on the surface, she remained undetected and escaped unscathed.

As the craft submerged there was a great deal of manual work to do. Here the U-bootmann is closing the exhaust outlets.

THE U-BOAT TEAM

At home in Germany, Gunther Prien and his crew were justifiably hailed as the great buccaneering heroes of the hour, but the bravery ascribed to them was not the most important quality required by a U-boat team. Clausdieter Oelschlagel considers that, first and foremost, a successful attack required discipline and team work.

'Everyone had to work together on a U-Boat. We all depended on each other. One wrong move and it could be disaster for all of us. It was not possible for someone to have a different opinion or to be stubborn or argue. You couldn't work like that. We all had our assigned tasks and we had to interact if we were going to be successful. We were a very young crew on our U-boat. None of the officers was more than twenty-four years old, and the rest of us were aged eighteen to twenty-two. The commander was only twenty-five. He was an excellent captain, very disciplined and keen to go into action, but not headstrong or overly daring. We all had a lot of respect for him and when you have a captain like that, discipline comes easily and routine goes smoothly.'

On board a U-boat out at sea, there was very little leisure for the crew, even during their off duty hours. Werner Karsties remembers how the engine crews were particularly busy.

'The engine crews were on duty in six hour shifts, six hours on watch, six hours off. During off duty time, they had to try and wash themselves, eat something or get some rest. The junior ratings, from ordinary rating up to to able rating, had to provide the officers with food. So there wasn't much time left over. If we had had a hit or suffered small scale damage, when a depth charge exploded close by, it sometimes happened that the water-level gauges for the tanks burst and had to be renewed or ball bearings had to be exchanged or

During the early part of the war approximately 50% of Allied ships sunk were attributed to U-boat action. The balance were mainly accounted for by the Luftwaffe.

repairs had to be carried out. That all had to be done during the off duty hours. If the others couldn't carry out a watch for any reason, then the off duty men had to fill in there as well. It was the same if there was a leak or we had been hit or whatever. We didn't get much time to ourselves and before we knew it, we were on duty again, looking for ships to attack!'

Clausdieter Oelschlagel describes the method U-boats used when making an attack.

'When a convoy was seen approaching, we used to dive. From then on, we used our ears. You can hear five times better under water than you can on the surface. We would listen to the ship's propellers humming above us and making a noise, and then we got the order to man battle stations. The commander sat up in the tower at the targeting periscope, which is in a cylinder. He could move it automatically with his feet, left and right, up and down. The first duty officer was beside him operating the equipment that made calculations for firing the torpedo. We could discharge salvos of two or four torpedoes - the boat had four tubes at the front and one at the rear in the stern. The attack rudder man was also up in the tower. Down in the control room, the chief engineer was waiting by the hatch to receive the commander's instructions - dive to twelve or fifteen metres or whatever. The order came to prepare tubes one and four, and when the commander was in the firing position he said: 'Fire!' and then tube one discharged.'

Once the torpedo was out and moving, the stop watch was started to check if the distance was approximately right. Sometimes, the torpedoes missed their targets, but if they exploded, then the U-boat crew knew they had another success. Hans Lange recalls that, even so, there was no joy in it.

'In my boat, no one shouted 'Hooray!' It was more like, 'Oh, God, the poor devils!'

Karl Ohrt remembers the tactics employed on his own U-boat.

'Mostly, we used to see the ships on the horizon when we were sailing on the surface. Along the line of the horizon, we saw a ship's mast or bridge or whatever. Then the type of ship was identified from a book, so that Germans didn't sink a German ship. We would try to

The training of U-boat crews had to be rapidly accelerated to make up for the huge losses. Inevitably this led to a decline in the quality of crews.

get up close and sink the ship whilst we were on the surface if it was possible, but if that wasn't possible, then we would get in front of it and try to make out its direction of travel - because they mostly sailed in a zig zag - in order to determine where we could strike at it. Working out the direction of Allied ships wasn't easy: they used to zig-zag across the ocean in order to frustrate us!'

Once the U-boat was submerged, a vital prerequisite to scoring a success was that everything should be done very quietly. "Run silent, run deep" has become a cliche but it is still the best advice for submariners. If the crewmen talked, it was in a whisper. Beneath the waves there were no loud commands, no sounds at all that could be heard by the enemy. Werner Ziemer remembers the efforts that had to be made on board a U-boat to remain undetected on a lurking U-boat.

'Air and electricity had to be used sparingly. There was hardly any movement into the boat, you didn't even eat, just drank a little. We had to take great care that we didn't rattle anything.'

Clausdieter Oelschlagel was first duty officer, manning the torpedo calculator during an attack.

Clausdieter Oelschlagel with fellow cadets at the beginning of the war. "Everyone had to work together on a U-Boat. We all depended on each other. One wrong move and it could be disaster for all of us."

'I used to stand beside the commander in the tower and enter his instructions into the torpedo calculator. These calculators became more and more complicated during the course of the War. Torpedoes didn't always run in a straight line, they ran out on a 90 degree path to the right and then out to the left. They were the 'LUT' or *Lageunhabhengieger* torpedoes which could be discharged from any position. Then there were torpedoes that turned in circles within the convoy.'

Once a hit had been made, the sounds made by a torpedoed ship breaking apart and sinking were fearful. They could be heard quite

Commander Weddigen, the great war U-boat ace who gave his name to the fledgling Third Reich training flotilla.

clearly through the water and the message from above was unmistakable. Werner Ritter von Voigtlander heard doomed ships in their death throes many times.

'Absolutely horrible, to tell the truth, were what the experts so nicely described as, 'breaking bulkheads and sinking noises'. When a steamer sank, the remaining air whistled through the gaps and it howled and cracked.'

A U-boat attack was made that much easier when the target was silhouetted against the sky and it was even clearer if another vessel in the convoy was already in flames and lit up the surrounding area. The submarine crew had no time to hang around to watch their handiwork once a hit had been scored. The first order of business was to escape and survive. Werner Ziemer recalls that in the U-boat war, the will to survive was the only emotion.

'It was us or them. We had no other choice. We couldn't stick ourselves in the sand to hide or crawl back to some safe position, like they could on land. Once you'd fired your torpedoes, the enemy knew you were there and had a pretty good idea of where you were, too.'

The torpedoes were at one and the same time a U-boat's deadly weapon and its Achilles heel. As the torpedoes sped towards their intended victim, the tell-tale pattern in the water gave the submarine's position away. From then on, it was a battle for survival, with the U-boat trying to outwit the enemy in a tense and deadly game of hide and seek. A pattern of depth charges laid in a spread could either destroy the U-boat or cause enough damage to force it to the surface and the waiting guns of the enemy. The hunter had become the hunted, and Kurt Wehling knew exactly when positions were reversed and the U-boat became the prey.

'We had surface torpedoes and you could see them, so the ships were warned. Also, torpedoes which didn't hit their targets gave us away because they were self-detonating. So if there was an explosion, nearby ships in the area knew there was a U-boat about. Then it started, the sirens sounded, we didn't hear them, but we knew they were giving the alarm. The destroyers started searching because the torpedoes had given us away. We dived straightaway and they searched for our U-boat with their equipment. The first depth charges dropped down and they exploded, you can hear that. If they are too close, the lights go out and the emergency lighting is switched on and depending on how the depth charges were falling, we would go down deeper still.'

The Radio operator on board a U-boat was particularly vulnerable when the depth charges started falling. He would give a verbal warning to the rest of the crew - 'Wasserbomben!' he said, 'Depth charges' but he would have to take his earphones off immediately, otherwise the noise that came through them would have burst his ear-drums.

If a U-boat managed to elude pursuit after the first depth charges were dropped, then a crew was not too badly off. Herr Guttmann records a lucky escape.

'We went down as fast as possible and all we noticed were the depth charges, there were no direct hits. And we had a terrific helmsman; the engines aren't used underwater, nothing, everything is quiet, and the helmsman was on the ball. There are naval maps on which the sea currents are drawn and he managed to turn the boat into deeper water with the currents, without any engine noise. And the deeper you are, the less effective the depth charges are, and because of that we got out unscathed.'

The real attrition in U-boat warfare came in a depth-charge chase. Then, the going really got tough. The U-boat would be constantly battered by shock waves, causing objects to fly around. The lights went out. For Herbert Lange, being depth-charged was a thoroughly nervewracking experience.

'When we were being hunted with depth charges, it tore at your nerves and spirit. It was terrible all right. And if anyone says that he wasn't afraid, he's lying. Depth charges were truly nerve-wracking. There were some comrades who were on the edge of cracking up; but we managed to control them each time.

'Twice, while I was on the U952, I experienced really heavy depth charge attacks, once off the coast of Greenland which lasted for about eight hours. Afterwards, our boat was so damaged that we could only just managed to creep home. During the hunt off

U-Boat Officer Clausdieter Oelschlagel in 1939, before his conscription to the German Navy. "It was depth charges here, depth charges there, depth charges everywhere. It ruined our nerves considerably."

Greenland, the torpedo tube became twisted, the attack periscope was faulty and various other things went wrong - there were cracks in the battery, gas formed because of the acid. We were in a terrible state. We were no longer fit for battle. That happened on our first voyage in the U952, but in a way it had a good effect. It welded the crew together, made us a team, we wanted to look after each other after that.'

'On the other occasion, in the Mediterranean, there was another hunt with depth charges which went on from early morning into the afternoon. We escaped from the field of the location soundings by means of a zig-zag trick. The Mediterranean is a very salty sea and there were layers of salt in which the soundings didn't work. We were lucky enough to sail into one of these salt layers and the enemy lost us.'

Herbert Lange remembers how important comradeship and discipline were when the boat was under attack.

'Everyone is at his station so that if a valve blows out or water breaks in, someone is always there to attempt to repair the damage. There are always men with strong nerves who lead those with weak

Operating the mass of machinery at the base of the Conning Tower required deft handling and constant attention. Note the swastika to the left of the crew man.

nerves by the hand, so to speak, and say, 'Keep calm! We'll get through it'. You have to be an optimist, especially if you're an officer, or a helmsman, because the crew look to you to see how you are behaving, whether you are trembling or not. You have to show yourself to be strong, be an example and say 'Come on lads, it's not that bad'.

Not all crewmen under the intense pressure of the depth charges were able to view the situation with such equanimity. One sailor on Werner von Voigtlander's U-boat lost his nerve completely.

Werner von Voigtlander, 2nd Duty Officer in the German navy.

'This man - he was one of our deep sea helmsmen - leapt up during a depth charge chase. We'd already been chased for more than a day, with a few interruptions, but the depth charges always resumed. It was just too much for this fellow. He leapt up and turned on the main pressurised air distributor, on the 'Christmas tree', we called it where all the distributors for the individual flooding chambers were - the pressure adjustment where there's a large wheel for the pressure adjustment. He wanted to get the boat up to the surface. We'd all have been goners if that had happened, but this man was so far out of his mind that he didn't care.'

'Fortunately, our control room mate Willy Difflueh, calmly tapped his skull with a spanner and he tipped over and collapsed, Willy turned the Christmas Tree off again, and we rolled this fellow head down in a hammock, tied it up and lay him down in a corner so that he couldn't do anything else stupid.'

The incident had caused problems inside the U-boat.

'After that, we had the problem of air in the diving chambers. There's water in them if you are under water, but when the boat moved this way or that way, then the air rumbled from the rear to the front and the noise of the water was horrible - you could hear it all over the place. Meanwhile, the enemy was up above, so we couldn't expel it through the main air duct because a huge bubble would rise to the surface and give our position away.'

'All the same, we managed to survive and the fellow who'd lost his nerve was later given a desk job at Brest with the flotilla there. Our commander hadn't reported him or anything, but officially the man could have been court-martialled. He wasn't any use, really, he was a bit weak. During the rest of the trip, he wasn't put on watch, but was given other jobs.'

Werner Voigtlander's own personal bugbear was the ASDIC sonar.

'We heard it go 'Ping ping . . ping ping! Then gravel would rattle across our deck, and we knew they'd got us again. We listened and heard 'Bloop!' and it gurgled a bit and the depth charges were on their way. As soon as the first charge exploded, we set our engines to half or full speed ahead. We brought the boat to the surface and the main bilge pumps switched on. That expelled the water which had forced its way into the boat.

'We used to count the depth charges. They came in a series of five...one, two, down came the third and the fourth. Once the fifth had exploded 'Whoomph!' then everything was switched off and we stood there in our socks going at 1.5 mph. Often, we thought: 'We're not going to get away! We've had it!' One hour, not even that, three quarters of an hour at full speed would take us seven and a half miles, and then the battery was empty. We crept along and it was a real game of cat and mouse.'

'They were up there, we were down below. We turned a little left here and little right, then left again and so on. Of course, we tried to deceive the enemy, pretend we'd sunk. We had a very small torpedo tube and we ejected a cartridge from it. This formed a spread of gas bubbles in the water and the ASDIC sonar could pick it up. We waited to see if the ruse had succeeded. It was a very tense moment, but if the gas bubbles had worked, we noticed, because the depth charges began to fall a few hundred metres astern. Then, we relaxed, we were happy.'

The routine did not always go smoothly, but Kurt Wehling remembers a number of counter measures which could be deployed by the crew on his U-boat to get out of trouble.

'If there were planes around chasing us when we surfaced at night, we would release air balloons with strips of silver foil attached. They floated just above the water with their strips of silver. It was like flypaper. The planes homed in on the silver strips and dropped their bombs on them instead of on us! There were lots of tricks we played!'

Spreading oil on the surface was a ploy the Germans used to make their pursuers think a U-boat had been sunk, since the one sure sign of a sinking when submarines were hit by depth charges was the escaping oil which came up to the surface automatically. Another tactic was designed to fool the hydrophones the British used early on in the War to detect submarines. The hydrophone, which was less effective than the later ASDIC, was a simple listening device designed to pick up propeller noise. It was very unreliable and could be used only if the ship on the search stopped its own propellers to listen for the U-boat's. The Germans found it easy to defeat the hydrophone in shallow waters: they just shut down their engines and lay silent on the seabed until the searchers went away.

Kurt Wehling, U-Boat volunteer. Wehling made 6 trips on U-73.

With the introduction of ASDIC the German response came in the form of the Bold (short for Kobold or "Goblin") capsule. Claus Orht remembers the deployment of this effective counter measure which was released through a mechanism known to the crews as a 'pill thrower'.

'If we were travelling under water and had been located - location was mostly carried out through soundings - a diesel engine makes a certain sound. The pill-thrower used to release a device which would imitate this sound. It was fired by the men in the engine room.'

Another effective counter measure in the face of the ASDIC submarine detector measure, was The Bold which was simply a mesh cylinder filled with Calcium Hydride which reacted with the surrounding salt water to produce a dense cloud of Hydrogen bubbles. These bubbles acted as a decoy which produced a false echo to ASDIC which given the primitve state of the equipment, appeared uncannily like a submarine.

It was a very simple idea, but like many simple ideas it worked brilliantly and it is one to which Claus Orht owes his life.

"The people on the ship hunting us would hear it and follow it, perhaps sailing in the direction of the 'pill' for twenty minutes or half an hour. By the time they realised they were on a wild goose chase, we'd sailed some distance ourselves and it was much more difficult for our pursuers to find us again.'

Escape from pursuing hunters was an ubearably tense

DEUTSCHES REICH

A wartime postage stamp which glorified the deeds of the U-boats.

experience which still resonates for Clausdieter Oelschlagel today:

'We sat totally still, almost on top of one another, mostly in the bow in order to keep the boat down. All you could do was to count the depth charges. When a depth charge went off, there was an enormous bang. The whole boat would leap up in one piece, dust flew everywhere, all the dust from behind the tubes flew out, the whole boat went 'Whoomp!' and then everything fell down again. There was just an unbelievable noise. Dreadful. The lights were turned out so as not to use additional electricity and we kept quiet so as not to use up too much oxygen. That was important too, not to use up too much oxygen in the longer diving periods and later when we were lying on the sea bed.'

The carbon dioxide that began to build up after a while had some alarming effects. At first, the boat was full of fresh air, but as the dive proceeded, that began to change.

'When the boat travelled on the surface masses of fresh, cool air came into the chamber at the very front, in the bow. The diesel engines running in the stern sucked the air through the entire boat. At the moment when there was an alarm dive the boat was full of fresh air, that was a great advantage: the air wasn't stale in the chambers but exactly as it was on deck. After a while, though, we used to start breathing very quickly because the build-up of carbon dioxide was affecting us. We began to feel very light headed, but we couldn't do anything about it. The ventilation couldn't be regulated so well below the surface. Normally, it was passed through some sort of a calcium filter and pumped out with a fan, but when you dived down to the sea bed with the enemy above you couldn't switch the equipment on.'

Once a U-boat had managed to elude its pursuers, any damage caused by the depth charges or the result of wear and tear had to be repaired out at sea. Werner Ziemer was literally in the middle of the

Atlantic Ocean when his boat developed rudder trouble.

'I volunteered for the job. The side rudder had started to make a noise and had to be greased. That could only be done on the surface. So I did it, and was awarded the Iron Cross, First Class for it. What I'd done, you see, was save the boat and the crew. But it was crazy, really. What would have happened if an air raid had taken place or a destroyer had appeared in front of the bow while I was doing the job? You don't think of that at the time, but afterwards, when you've got time to reflect, you realise that the boat would have had to dive and I would have been left floundering in the ocean. That actually happened once, when we'd been attacked by gunfire. Two members of the crew lay dead on deck. Heaven knows if they were really dead or not. Considering what happened soon after, I hope they were.

They collapsed up there, one of them had been shot in the head and the other one fell over. We never saw them again because they were still on the upper deck when we had to dive. The others came storming over because the alarm had been given. They jumped down the hatch, the hatch was closed and the boat dived. But when you were out on deck, you tried not think about that sort of thing happening. You did your duty and that was the first consideration.'

Despite their vulnerable, essentially isolated position when at war, U-boat crews enjoyed, or rather assumed, privileges not open to their compatriots in other services. Soldiers, for example, were very carefully monitored for correct behaviour. Any sign of deviation from the strict Nazi line, the slightest hint of criticism or dissent, was heavily punished. U-boat crews, on the other

Von Voigtlander's Prisoner of War Index Card.

hand, were much freer to express themselves and on Werner von Voigtlander's boat, they felt a sort of comradeship with their British opponents.

'Just imagine, we used to sing our English shanties on duty! 'Rolling Home' or 'Blow the Man Down! Even Adolf Hitler couldn't stop us doing it. Before the War, I had served time in a juvenile prison because we had copied English jazz records and so on, when we were at school. Jazz was forbidden, of course. But we had some of these same

The U-boat crews were supplied with the very best provisions which the hard pressed German war machine could supply.

records, and we played them on board, with great enthusiasm. The Nazis could interfere with us only when we were in harbour. I remember that we were once berthed in Wilhelmshaven when a Nazi Party official, a political guidance officer, came on board. The Nazis must have known what we did at sea, because they didn't trust the U-boat men past the end of their noses. Anyway, this official got short shrift from our captain. He said: 'You know what, you're in the way. You have no life jacket, you have no respirator kit, you have no idea - go back home we can't use you!' I was amazed. It was a very brave thing to do, but our captain just bundled that official off the ship, and sent him unceremoniously home.'

Even when in port, U-boat crews had a tendency to break the rules. Claus Ohrt once helped smuggle a small dog on board.

'We had a dog when were sailing out on commander training even though it was verboten to have dogs on board. We had sailed back from Gotenhaven, it was night time, evening and a small dog, a puppy, crossed our path. He kept following us, whimpering. We couldn't just leave him, so my mate held the dog when we passed the guards and gave in our cards. They didn't notice, and we brought him on board the boat. We managed to keep him for six weeks. No one knew he was there, not an officer nor an NCO. No one knew we had a little dog up front in the crew room. It couldn't go on, of

Heinz Reiner, left, with comrade in 1940. Reiners was sunk three times during a mission to Narvik. "Three times into the ice cold water up there in Norway!"

course, and one day the dog was discovered. But we decided to have a souvenir and took him up on deck where everyone who had had anything to do with the dog, sat down, and we had our photograph taken. The next day we had to give him in. But by then, he was getting too big for us anyway.'

When a U-boat sailed into harbour after completing its mission, there would be a pennant flying saying how many tons of shipping its crew had sunk. If the tonnage was sufficiently high, the commander was awarded the Knight's Cross. There was a band playing. The girls from the Bund Deutscher Madchen - the female version of the Hitler Youth - were there to greet the returning heroes. Heinz Reiners felt proud when his boat sailed in.

'We were given extra pay for being on board, working machinery, a danger allowance, a diving allowance, a basic allowance, and our regular pay. We were heroes, no doubt of that. So when we sailed in, we lifted the roof in the harbour. We went a bit wild.'

LIFE ABOARD

It was understandable. U-boat crews were young men, often very young men, operating at sea in a state of extreme tension. Life on board was hard and often uncomfortable. Werner Ziemer experienced some very cramped conditions.

'We were rarely able to take off our clothes, there was one bunk for two men. We also had to take several tons of stores with us and they were stowed away all over the place. When we sailed out of the harbour there were torpedoes between the bunks and on the flooring. The table was laid on top of them and that was how we ate our meals.'

The food on board the submarines was good, better than it was in wartime Germany. One man who was well placed to know was Rudolph Guttmann, a butcher in peacetime life, who was a cook (known as a "sutje") on the U-boats. Later, Guttmann went on to become a cook on the famous battle cruiser Gneisenau.

'No one complained about the food on the U-boats. There was certainly enough of it. We were spoiled, I suppose - we received 'Status 1' food rations. Unfortunately, it all tasted of gasoline, but still, no one complained. I didn't have much space for my kitchen. It was the size of a small corner and there, I had to cook meals for forty-eight men. It's amazing what you can do when you have to!

I did most of the work on my own. The crew used to peel potatoes, I didn't have to do that. The potatoes, wash the vegetables a bit, they did that. But mostly it was tinned food. We had fresh food only during the first two weeks of an operation. After that it was just tins. The tin opener was my most important tool! If it was broken, I used to use an axe. Chop, chop, chop! but it worked! We had fresh water tanks, there was more than enough drinking water. During attacks, I used to stay in the galley - it was my battle station, so to speak and everyone remained at their battle stations. If we were submerged and

I wanted to fetch twenty or thirty cans for meals from the rear, then I had to inform the control room and they balanced the weight of the boat, pressed water from the front to the back or whatever, because if three or four men went to the rear without telling anyone, the boat would tip over. That didn't happen. The boat floated exactly right, because the weight was adjusted back and forth according to where the men were. Food was stored everywhere. In the galley, in the toilets at the front, they were crammed full of provisions too. Things hung here and there, shoved between the metal girders and as I said, in the end it all absorbed the smell and tasted like gasoline.'

Clausdieter Oelschlagel found the food was good, gasoline or no gasoline.

'It was terrific! We always ate at the table with a knife and fork and so on. No spooning things out of tins like some of our comrades elsewhere. In any case, the hardships endured by soldiers in Russia were much worse than those we had to undergo, by and large.'

Crews regarded their U-boats as home, and Hans Lange was very upset when his own craft was destroyed in a bombing raid at Toulon.

'Our boat lay in the shipyard, high up in the dock at Toulon and the crew was on leave. British bombers came over and it was badly damaged. We received a telegram telling us to return to Toulon immediately. We went down to the harbour and saw our boat damaged and lying on its side, then I have to say, we had tears in our eyes. The boat was our home. It had brought us safely through five operational trips against the enemy and seeing it in that state hurt a lot.'

The German submarines were basically very wet, and crews had to live with constant damp.

'We used to call our boat a 'stalagmite cave'. It was particularly damp at the front section, in the bow, where we kept all the chains and other equipment for transport and bringing the torpedoes into position. Yet, it was wet all right. You got soaking wet on the bridge, if there was a light storm. We found it very difficult to get clothes and such things dry. All we could do was keep on wearing our wet clothes and wait until they dried out on us. Fortunately, we were all young and just shrugged it off. That was the way it was and there was nothing much we could do about it.'

Crews washed themselves in sea water desalinated in the engine room, if they washed at all. Washing was something of a luxury on board a U-boat. So was shaving. Many of the German submariners grew beards, which gave them a rather jaunty appearance when they were on leave, but was actually a matter of necessity. While on board, they were like troglodytes, sometimes living for months without seeing daylight. Their world beneath the sea was a malodorous world of sweat, noise, oil and heat. Werner Ziemer put it bluntly: 'The air stinks down there. It stinks!'

Diving could be another unsettling experience. The tower hatch on the U-boat was closed and in a very short time, water was already splashing over it and the craft was on its way down. Clausdieter Oelschlagel still remembers what it was like:

'When the U-boat was going to dive, you heard the alarm. A switch was thrown, men scrambled through all the rooms and the lights flashed off and on. Until then, we'd been using the diesel engines, but now, the diesels were stopped and the connection shaft to the e-engine was disengaged. The e-engine was switched on and

Heinz Reiners' Narvik badge. "I experienced this myself: survivors, men swimming in the water would be machine-gunned."

we went over immediately to full speed.

'That was especially important when enemy planes were around. When they attacked or were visible on our tail, we managed to dive down to 50 or 100 metres within 45 seconds from the time the alarm was given. But if someone was too late in recognising the plane or the plane swept out of the clouds on an attack course, then it was hair-raising. In some instances it was better to stay on the surface and try to out manoeuvre the bombs. When the boat dived, then we normally went down at an angle of 25 to 30 degrees. Sometimes it was more, and then everything that was lying around loose tumbled down around us, including food. There were two deep sea helmsmen, a chief engineer, and there were deep sea rudders at the front and the rear. One was turned upwards, the other downwards and we manoeuvred partly with the engine. We could dive only when we were at full speed.'

With all these pressures and discomforts to contend with, it was hardly surprising that once in harbour, U-boat crews often went to extremes. The authorities ashore were well aware of it.

'Onshore, we used to be pursued by 'watch dogs' as we called them, the field soldiers or the gendarmerie. Their job was to make sure that we didn't give them the slip. If you travelled to Brest on the train, there were always controls in Metz because everyone knew we were going to play the fool.'

Heinz Reiners believes this wild behaviour was justified.

'It was like this. We never really knew whether we were going to get home or not. We were a bit superstitious, I suppose. Once a trip was over or almost over, we never said 'We'll be home in three days.' We might not get home, we knew that. We heard that this boat was overdue, that boat was overdue. No one knew what had happened to them. It could have been us. So we let loose once we'd reached safe harbour. We went with girls of easy virtue because we had plenty of money and wanted to forget what we'd been through. It seemed the best way, the most obvious way. We often got drunk, too. That's the way it was. But at heart, it wasn't what we wanted. We wanted some lovely girl to fall in love with, a nice respectable girl who'd love us in return. But all we had were girls you had to pay and in the end it just made you sick. It's all right for a while, but eventually that way of life just made you sick.'

In 1939, 1940 and on into 1941, the German U-boats enjoyed great success. The conquests of Norway and France by June 1940 had increased their range by opening up harbours beyond Germany as new bases of operation. The U-boats took full advantage and between June and October 1940, they sank two hundred and seventy four merchant ships, for the loss of only six submarines. The new bases on the French coast enabled the U-boats to range much further into the Atlantic where they posed an even greater threat than before to the vital supplies coming across the ocean from America. This was an indispensable lifeline. If it were cut or crippled, it was perfectly possible that Britain could have been starved into submission.

Wolfgang Luth was one of the most successful U-boat commanders, a tough breed who were revered and respected in their homeland.

Rudolf Guttmann recalls the tactics that were used when hunting convoys.

'Our job was to sail up and down through a grid square. Up and down, up and down and so on and continually watch, watch, watch. If we saw any ships, we reported them to Admiral Donitz at U-boat headquarters. There was a large map there and on it, they recorded our sightings. Convoys were reported by more than one U-boat. This way, it was possible to determine in which direction the convoy was sailing. U-boats from other areas were directed towards the convoy.'

The British convoy system nevertheless afforded some protection for the ships it comprised, and together with other anti-submarine tactics, obliged the U-boats to alter their own strategy. They

Rudolf Gutmann, a U-Boat crewman. Gutmann was a galley cook, preparing meals alone for 48 men.

concentrated instead on lone ships or stragglers and if they attacked convoys, they attacked at night.

This put the lookouts on the convoy ships at a great disadvantage. In the early stages of the War, convoys still relied mainly on visual observation to detect submarines. That could be difficult enough by daylight, but at night it was almost impossible. In the dark, the low profile of a U-boat could easily be missed. Consequently, the tactic of attacking by night was extremely successful. Enormous tonnages were sunk in this way.

One U-boat commander, Otto Kretschmer of the U99, became a submarine ace, sinking around 267,000 tons in all. During one voyage alone, he accounted for seven ships. Kretschmer, who was awarded the Knight's Cross with Oak Leaves and Swords for his exploits, was the first German submarine commander to exceed the quarter million mark and achieved it within a fairly short time: before 27 March 1941, when the U99 was captured by two British destroyers and he became a prisoner for the rest of the War.

THE ALLIED EXPERIENCE

> "YOU CAN GET TERRIBLY ANXIOUS. ARE THEY GOING TO DROP DEPTH CHARGES OR NOT? YOU DON'T KNOW UNTIL IT HAPPENS."
>
> **HEINRICH SCHMIDT**

Some two months before the capture of Kretschmer, a Welsh collier, the 2,473-ton Sarastone, en-route from Lisbon to England caused serious damage to a U-boat and sailed on without completing the kill only because the captain, John Herbert, was under orders not to risk his cargo.

'The chief engineer came to me and explained that our boilers had blown. 'We shall have to leave the convoy and take a chance on our own,' he said. Our engines would not carry us faster than two knots. So while the rest of the ships steamed on, we altered course and headed for Lisbon. Two days later, the second officer on the bridge shouted down the voice pipe to my cabin: 'There's something on the horizon that I don't like, sir'. When I got to the bridge, I saw what appeared to be a mast about three miles distant. Then, I saw it rise higher, until the streaming conning tower of a U-boat emerged. I put Action Stations on, and swung the ship round to bring the U-boat astern. But while she was still lying on our quarter, she fired, the shot falling off our starboard side. It was a warning to stop. We kept on. The U-boat's speed was about fifteen knots and she overhauled us rapidly for ten minutes, but without firing. Then, when she was about 4,000 yards away, she loosed five shoots. We held our fire. We had only a twelve-pounder, but I'd already talked over with my naval gunner, James O'Neill, what we'd do in such a predicament and our plans were made. The U-boat was getting closer and closer. I held my breath waiting for the moment when we could open fire with hope of damaging her Her shells fell uncomfortably close to our ship. The submarine was about two thousand yards off when O'Neill opened fire. His first

Once the craft had submerged, controlling the dive planes was a vital task which required a deft touch and constant watchfulness.

shot fell short, but in perfect line. He fired again and scored a direct hit.

'We all cheered. I shouted 'Go on, O'Neill, give it to him!' His second shot fell at the base of the aft gun, putting it out of action and causing yellow smoke to rise in a cloud. Our third and fourth shots were near misses, but the fifth burst twenty feet abaft the first hit, and the yellow smoke now turned black. After that, we sailed on. The U-boat was still firing at us, but the Germans had only one gun left now, and we got away.'

The U-boats were chased by British submarines as well as by

surface vessels and the undersea duels did not always go the Germans' way. The Royal Navy's H.M. Submarine Salmon, which sank the battleship Blücher in Oslofjord in 1940 during the German invasion of Norway, was somewhere in the North Sea on 4 December 1939 when it came across a U-boat on the surface. A member of the Salmon's crew described the action in a letter home.

'It was a bright sunny day, two o'clock in the afternoon. This U-boat was chugging along on the surface about two miles ahead of us. We got into position and let go our 'tin fish' in quick succession. One of them got her right amidships and cut her clean in half. She went straight to the bottom. We surfaced and had a quick look round for survivors, but there were none. All we saw was the top half of a man's body with a life jacket holding it up. Pretty grim, but who knows how many innocent women and children might have been killed by that U-boat had we missed her.'

Later the same month, the Salmon sighted the German steamer Bremen and prepared to attack. Then, the steamer's air escort was sighted.

'We sighted the steamer during the afternoon and prepared to stop

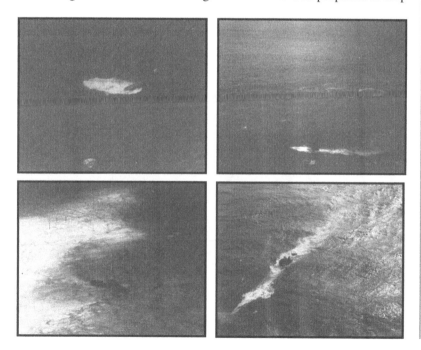

Part of a sequence of stills which capture the last moments of U172.

her by firing a shell across her bows. Now, according to international law, a merchant must not be sunk by a man-of-war unless that man-of-war can rescue her entire crew. So the position was that we must tell her to stop and force her to alter her course towards England, but under no circumstances must we attempt to sink her. We came to the surface, manned the gun, loaded it and were about to fire when we noticed that the Bremen was escorted by half a dozen aircraft. As we are fair game for anyone when we're on the surface, we dived in about thirty seconds and left the gun loaded, the gun crew flying down the hatch as if the devil was after them. If we had fired that gun, I should certainly be dead now. Those Luftwaffe aircraft would certainly have found and bombed us. This area is full of enemy craft, as we are just outside their base, and it was by the grace of God that we have not been sighted and sunk. Luckily, neither the Bremen nor the aircraft saw us, so we stayed down until she was well past, then came to the surface again and wirelessed her position, course and speed to the Admiralty.'

The Admiralty never caught up with the Bremen. She sank in

The Naxos detector was one of the many successful measures introduced in the attempt to restore the technological balance, but it was always a case of too little too late as the Allied technology continued to race ahead.

The surface vessels of the Kreigsmarine and her Italien allies played their part too. Mine laying was a highly effective activity. This photograph from Signal Magazine depicts an Italien crew at work in the Mediterranean in 1941.

1941 after a disgruntled German seaman set her on fire.

The United States was not yet a combatant, but the American policy of 'all aid short of war' laid her ships open to U-boat attack. One of them was the destroyer USS Kearney, which was damaged by a torpedo on 17th October 1941, but survived. The USS Reuben James was not so lucky. On 31st October, with four other destroyers, she was escorting a North Atlantic convoy 600 miles west of Ireland when she was torpedoed and sunk by the U562.

The boat on which Werner Ziemer served typified the wide range the Germans submarines were able to enjoy at this time.

'We sailed from Trondheim on our first operation against the enemy, sailing between the Shetland and Faroe Islands. We weren't chased with depth charges, we got through without a problem; we got hold of a convoy off the coast of England. Our boat sailed on the surface through the escort and we then chose the individual 'pots', following the convoy together with other boats up as far as Newfoundland. By the time we got there, the convoy had ceased to exist, it was destroyed. After that, we sailed back to the frontline docks in Brest and the 1st U-Flotilla. We had a short home leave, we were newly equipped and the boat was overhauled before we undertook our second operation down to the south Atlantic through the Bay of Biscay. We didn't get far before we sank a frigate and a corvette off the coast of Portugal.'

By this time, though, British anti-submarine tactics had caught up with Ziemer's U-boat.

'We were still off the Portuguese coast when we got it in the neck, and how! We were attacked by Sunderlands, the RAF flying boats, and when they attacked, all we could see was a wall of flame from left to right, from one end of the wing to the other. The Sunderland shot one of our deep sea bunkers to pieces. A deep sea bunker was an oil bunker that was used later as a water bunker, a deep sea bunker, when the oil had been used up. Because of that, we left a telltale trail of oil which was clearly seen by the aircraft above, and we were chased with depth charges for a whole day. Our commander was getting tired of all this and turned our boat round, through 360 degrees. 'This is ridiculous' he said. So he mixed the old trail of oil with a new one and then they lost us. After the attack by the planes we had two dead and sixteen men injured and had to sail back into the frontline docks at Brest.'

Germany's legendary Type VII class submarines did most of the fighting in the U-boat war. They were ideally suited for it. The Type VIIs, the convoy-combat boats, had a low conning tower, only 5.2metres above the surface, and were hard to see even in daylight. At night, they were practically invisible, especially when viewed bow-on. These submarines could dive in less than thirty seconds and it was no effort for them to reach depths of one hundred metres. They could make double that depth if necessary. The depth and endurance of the Type VIIs were twice that of their Allied counterparts. These U-boats had a range of seven thousand miles, doing twelve knots on the surface, and could travel ninety miles at four knots when submerged. This was steady, but Herbert Lange found it very slow.

'The electric engine could travel at a top speed of only 8 knots maximum when we were submerged. At full speed, that meant the battery only had enough power for ninety minutes. We had to be careful, but by going at a slow or at least minimal speed, we could hold out for twenty four hours or more. Of course, we had to surface some time, and that was when the enemy had his chance to chase and destroy us.'

Despite the disadvantages, Lange believes the Type VII class were much better suited to submarine warfare than the Italian or British submarines, even though these were outwardly superior.

'Basically, the German U-Boats were not comparable to the Italian, which lay heavily in the water, or even the English ones. Our boats were battle ships, so to speak. Later, there were bigger boats of approximately 1000 tonnes, which made longer trips to the Far East. They were also more cumbersome and practically unusable in a convoy battle because they were that much larger. Their losses were correspondingly higher. They were more awkward when diving and if they were hit, then that was the end of them. Mostly, there was nothing left. Our Class VII boats were substantially more stable and more robust. The British were afraid of them. They regarded our U-boats with fear and loathing. To them, I suppose, submarine warfare appeared ruthless, cunning and impersonal.'

The Class VIIs certainly had remarkable endurance, as was demonstrated by the U331 after it had torpedoed the battleship Barham off Crete on 25 November 1941 and was forced by British depth charges to go deeper than any U-boat was safely designed to go. Heinrich Schmidt was on board.

'We received a message one afternoon. It read: 'Three English battle-ships are sailing out of Malta, the Queen Elizabeth, the Barham and the Valiant.' They were protected by eight destroyers

The last moments of HMS Barham sunk by U331 in the Mediterranean on November 25th 1941.

The "Wagtail" gyrocopter was a useful addition to the U-boat armoury which greatly extended the range at which targets could be spotted. The operator was in grave danger in the event that the submarine had to crash dive.

and RAF aircraft and sailed across our tubes in the area near Tobruk. We didn't notice them. The ships didn't notice either that we were so close to them, just around seven hundred metres away. We knew why these battleships were there: they wanted to put an end to Rommel's African campaign. Our commander was at the periscope and saw the English fleet. Their signal flags were hoisted and that meant 'Attack'. Then, the Barham turned away and all we saw was a white-grey wall. The commander ordered all four tubes to be made ready, which we did and then we fired a salvo of four.

'We hit the Barham from a distance of five to seven hundred metres with a salvo of four torpedoes. The third 'eel', as we called our torpedoes, penetrated the Barham's ammunition chamber and the ship sank within a few minutes. It was sad. We heard later that 846 people on board had been drowned. After the Barham was hit, the Valiant approached, intending to ram us, but at that moment the Barham exploded and she had to turn away.'

The attack, though successful, had caused the U331 problems even though the explosion on board the Barham saved the submarine.

'Because we now had four empty torpedo tubes, we weren't heavy enough. We didn't flood them immediately, as we should have done, and that's why we went up to a periscope depth of 13.5 metres. But when the Valiant had to turn away, we escaped being rammed. The Valiant fired at us, but way over our heads because the angle was too steep. Finally, we escaped by going down to extreme depths, but it was risky. Everyone was ordered to the bow to add their weight and we dived. The depth pressure gauge hadn't been switched on and the commander didn't know how deep we were. It read sixty metres, and when we switched on the depth pressure gauge, we discovered that it was more than 200 metres. That's why we were lucky enough to get out of it. After that, we didn't hear the depth charges the British fired at us. We were too deep for that. But we'd done our bit to help Rommel's African campaign and we'd got away with it. Afterwards, we received a confirmation from Grand Admiral Dönitz that we had been down deeper than any other VIIC boat. Late that evening, we started to surface. We went up a metre at a time and surfaced at 11 o'clock at night. We saw an empty Mediterranean, the battle ships were no longer to be seen. The sinking of the Barham was kept secret by the English Admiralty until two months later, when they reported it to be lying at a depth of 31,300 metres in the Mediterranean. The other two battleships, the Queen Elisabeth and the Valiant were holed by Italian one-man U-Boats off the coast of Alexandria and were out of action one year.'

The U331 survived, but it had been a very dangerous maneouvre. U-boats going down that far risked a massive build-up of pressure that could cause the hull to implode. Even worse was the nightmare of being trapped alive on the floor of the ocean. The only prospect then was slow death by asphyxiation.

Heinrich Schmidt lived to tell the tale because the U331 managed to get back to the surface late the same evening.

> "IT IS A BITTER AND SAD NOISE WHEN THE DESTROYERS AND DEPTH CHARGES ARE COMING."
> **HEINZ REINERS**

THE ARCTIC CONVOYS

The challenges of the Atlantic and the water around Britain were daunting enough, but they had nothing on the conditions the U-boats found when they opened a campaign in Arctic waters in June 1941. Extending operations as far north as this was occasioned by the Allied convoys that were carrying aid and supplies to the Russian ports of Murmansk and Archangel.

The Arctic waters were the most dangerous and inhospitable in the world. There was the unending, numbing nightmare of fog, ice, blizzard, heaving seas and the freezing, howling winds of Arctic storms. New fears were added to the already fraught lives of those on board the U-boats: frostbite, or drowning in seas so cold that simply falling in was a guarantee of death.

The ports of departure for Allied ships on the Murmansk run were Loch Ewe in northern Scotland, 1,600 miles distant or Rekjavik in Iceland 1,500 miles away. Most of the distance was under U-boat surveillance or attack and not all the Allied merchantmen sailing it were given protective escorts. In these circumstances, the chances of a convoy reaching its destination intact were poor. Or, as Prime Minister Winston Churchill put it: 'The operation is justified if half gets through.'

Ultimately, the Murmansk convoys carried more than 22,000 aircraft, 375,000 trucks, 8,700 tractors, 51,500 jeeps, 1,900 locomotives, 343,700 tons of explosives, a million miles of field telephone cable, together with millions of shoes, rifles, machine guns, tyres, radio sets and other equipment - and as a result kept Russia in the war. This achievement was enabled only by gargantuan effort and at tremendous risk. Most of the convoy ships were carrying some form of armament, so that a torpedo from a

submarine or a stick of bombs from Luftwaffe aircraft could mean instant, total destruction for both the vessel and its crew. Most merchant ships were too slow to outrun the German U-boats and the early convoys were too lightly armed to put up an adequate defence.

This did not mean that they were sitting ducks for the prowling submarines. During the voyage of Convoy PQ-16 in May 1942, a submarine had its conning tower blown clean away by one of the ships, Expositor, and the U88, U589 and U457 were sunk by the convoy escorts. However, the Murmansk was not the sort of battlefield in which either side had the advantage for long. Both Heinz Reiners and Werner Karsties were on U-boats seconded to hunt Allied ships in the fearful Arctic environment. Both had their successes. Reiners' U-boat claimed a destroyer and a merchant ship and Karsties took part in a torpedo attack against a large refrigerator vessel.

Karsties' U-boat had been searching for prey for three or four weeks, without any result, and the refrigerator ship looked

An Obermachinst at work diagnosing problems and carrying out running repairs and maintenance.

I. Die Heimkehr

2 Die Besatzung ist auf dem Vorschiff angetreten und „macht sich schön" für die Rückkehr in die Zivilisation. Die Kappen werden so korrekt wie möglich auf den wild gewachsenen Schopf — Kokarde genau über der Nasenspitze! gesetzt und der Stolz der Heimkehrer, der Bart, wird noch einmal aufgewirbelt

3 Langsam gleitet jetzt das U-Boot an den Anlegeplatz heran, der Obersteuermann leitet das Manöver, die Besatzung steht auf dem Vorschiff in Reih und Glied, und Hunderte von Zuschauern, sind zur Begrüßung gekommen. Die Kapelle spielt „Denn wir fahren gegen England . . .", gleich fliegen die Halteleine hinüber

1 Die Stürme und Gefahren des Atlantik liegen nach Wochen erfolgreicher Feindfahrt — neun Siegeswimpel sind die Zeichen —, hinter den Männern des U-Bootes. Sie winken hinüber zum Land, zu den Kameraden der Küstenverteidigung, und der Signalgast beantwortet den Willkommensgruß der Signalstation. Ein großes Sicherungsfahrzeug (rechts) hat das U-Boot weit vor der Küste in seinen Schutz genommen und gleitet es nun in den Hafen

4 Das Boot ist vertäut, und nach vielen Wochen Feindfahrt: ferne Lande oft in Sicht, doch nie betreten — kommt das erste Stückchen Heimat an Bord, ein schmales Brot

5 Der langersehnte Augenblick ist da: wieder einmal an Land! Junge Mädchen schmücken die Heimkehrer mit Blumen

U-BOOT-
Stützpunkt am Atlantik

PK-Kriegsberichter Hanns Hubmann schildert in den folgenden acht Kapiteln seiner Bilderzählung die Heimkehr eines deutschen U-Boots zu seinem Stützpunkt an der Atlantikküste, die kurzen Wochen der Erholung für die Besatzung und der Reparatur für das Boot und die neue Ausfahrt gegen den Feind

I. The Homecoming. An extended feature in the form of a photographic journal detailing the fortunes of a U-boat returning from a combat patrol in the Atlantic.

II. BACK TO BEER, PAY AND SOAP

Back to beer, pay and soap!...among other things. The homecoming crew enjoys the higher standard of provisions which were provided for the U-boat men in recompense for the privations and dangers of their regular duties. The propaganda article has neglected to list the main priority of many returning crew men which was to find a willing woman as quickly as possible. The inevitable consequence of these frequent liasons with French and German prostitutes was the wide spread instance of venereal disease among U-boat crews.

II. Wieder Bier, Post, Sold und Seife

6 Der Flottillenchef, der als erster an Bord gekommen war, hat die Besatzung vom Anlegeplatz weg mitgenommen in die Kantine und seinen Jungens ein frische kühles Bier (aus Bremen!) kredenzt, ein lang entbehrter Genuß

Jetzt ist der Höhepunkt der Begrüßungsfeier gekommen, die Postverteilung Zwei Kameraden verteilen die Briefe und Päckchen, die sich seit Monaten hier angesammelt haben. Bald ...

8 ... ist jeder in seine Briefe vertieft, freut sich über gute Nachrichten, wie hier der Jüngste mit seinem „U-Boots-Bart". Seine Schwester hat im letzten Urlaub, ... na das gehört ja eigentlich nicht hierher!

9 Nach der Begrüßungsfeier wieder auf dem Boot, gibt der Rechnungsführer den Wehrsold aus, der sich in der langen Zeit der Feindfahrt angesammelt hat. Eine prall gefüllte Kasse ist an Bord gekommen ...

10 Und die schöne Bärte fallen Scheren und Messern zum Opfer

III. THE DOCK REFIT BEGINS
The process of turning a U-boat round for its next mission was a lengthy and involved tasks which required detailed planning and effort.

III. Die Werftzeit beginnt

11 Neue Arbeit an Bord. Das Boot wird ausgeräumt. Der I.W.O. (Erster Wachoffizier) benachigt dem Torpedomixer, daß im Verlauf der Feindfahrt alle die „Aale" verschossen wurden, deren Bücher jetzt an Land gehen

12 In den Bauch des U-Bootes hinunter steigt eine Kommission von Werftbeamten, die an Ort und Stele mit dem L.I. (Leitenden Ingenieur) besprechen, welche Reparaturen zu machen sind

14 Kurze Zeit später werden in dem historischen Besprechungssaal, dessen Wände die Schattenrisse französischer Seehelden schmücken, zwischen Werftleitung, Kommandanten und Flottilleningenieur die Termine für die Reparaturen festgelegt, während . . .

13 Aus allen Luks kommt das Inventar des Bootes an . . . Werkzeug, Kisten und Kasten! Smutje stellt sein ganzes Geschirr durch das Kombüsenluk ins Freie!

IV. IN THE CONCRETE U-BOAT PENS

The heavily re-enforced concrete pens which housed the U-boat fleets were essential to protect the refitting craft from allied air raids which grew more and more frequent as the war progressed. The immense complex, built to house the 6th and 7th U-Flotillas at Saint-Nazaire, is the best surviving example of these structures. Capable of accommodating 20 U-Boats, it boasted 14 deep water chambers, some of which could be drained and used as dry docks for more difficult repairs. Built from enormous quantities of heavily reinforced concrete, with massively thick walls and roof, armoured doors and anti –aircraft gun platforms, the St Nazaire pens constituted a self-contained fortress within which boats could be re-provisioned, maintained, repaired, refuelled, re-armed in safety.

IV. In den Docks aus Beton

16 Das riesige Tor einer Einfahrt zu der Bisonbunker-Anlage ist geöffnet, und das U-Boot gleist langsam, von Schleppern geschoben, in das bombensichere, von der Organisation Todt erbaute riesige Werk. Dort wird das Boot aus dem Wasser gehoben und im Trockendock für die notwendig gewordenen Reparaturarbeiten aufgestellt

17 Meterdicke Decken und Wände aus Eisenbeton schützen die U-Boote in den Bunkern vor jeder Störung durch englische Bomben. Der Engländer kommt zwar immer wieder, doch immer wieder ist es nur die französische Zivilbevölkerung, deren Häuser den Bomben zum Opfer fallen

18 Sicher aber liegt das Boot im betongepanzerten Dock. Alle Ver langen sind entfernt, weil Scharen von Werftarbeitern, sind am Werk auch, die geringste Kleinigkeit, die auf der langen Fahrt durch N genutzen oder Feindeinwirkung beschädigt wurde, zu ersetzen oder auszube

19 Der Obermaschinist des Bootes überwacht neben den Werftingenieuren den Fortgang der Arbeiten an den Auspuffrohren des Dieselmotors

20 Auch ein Teil der Besatzung bleibt ständig in der Nähe ihres Bootes u hilft mit an den Reparaturen. Hier sitzen die Maschinengasten auf d Fendern, entrosten Maschinenteile und bemalen sie mit neuer Schutzfa

V. Bericht und dann . . .

21 Der Kommandant, ein junger Kapitänleutnant, der schon im Spanienkrieg als Seeflieger eingesetzt war, erstattet seinem Befehlshaber, Admiral Dönitz, Bericht. Er beschreibt den Verlauf der Fahrt, die Gefechte und alle Versenkungen auf das genaueste

22 Und der Admiral, schon im Weltkrieg bewährter Unterseebootkommandant, macht seine Einwendungen, gibt Ratschläge und sieht für sich und seinen Admiralstab aus den Berichten seiner Kommandanten, die nach jeder Feindfahrt zu ihm kommen, Erfahrungen für die Kriegsführung

23 U-Boot-Besatzungen und Werftarbeiter, sie alle wohnen in riesigen Bunkern, genau so beschützt wie die Boote. Sie beschwören beim ...

nun ist der Augenblick gekommen, an dem die Auszeichnungen, die der Führer der Besatzung verliehen hat, überreicht werden sollen. Musterung in Blau ist befohlen. Und die U-Boot-Männer, sonst in ihrer Ölkleidung, verwandeln sich wieder in richtige blaue Jungens'. Der Heizer (Bild links) soll ebenfalls das E.K. bekommen, hat aber bis nur ein paar Minuten im Revier gelegen. Damit es noch rechtzeitig ..., hilft ihm der I.W.O.! Der Jüngste der Besatzung, schon lange ohne seinen blonden Bart, hat wie alle Kameraden die seidenen Mützenbänder schon gebügelt und um die Mütze gelegt (Bild rechts)

V. THE REPORT AND THEN.... *Dönitz took a very close interest in the detail of the U-boat operations and personally debriefed as many returning commanders as possible. He understood the enormity of the task and the huge dangers which the crews faced treated them with great respect and informality even allowing the commanders to address him by the German personal pronoun "du".*

VI. THE REWARD
The successful crew receives decorations and wards and a welcome period of leave. Unless the boat was seriously damaged and needed extensive repair this all too brief respite would be quickly followed by another patrol.

..VI. die Belohnung

25 „Mensch, Knoop, Sie haben ja die Mütze wie einen Südwester auf!" Der Funkmaat M. inspiziert bei der Musterung zur Ordensverleihung die Männer, die in der ersten Reihe antreten sollen, weil ihnen der Flotillenchef die Eisernen Kreuze überreichen wird

26 Er selbst, der Funkmaat, steht dann ganz vorne vor der Front, und der Flotillenchef, Ritterkreuzträger und erfolgreicher U-Bootkommandant, steckt ihm als einzigem der Besatzung nach dieser Fahrt das E. K. I an die Brust

27 Und Knoop, der Signalgast mit dem „Südwester", freut sich sehr, als der Flotillenchef ihm als zwölftem das Band des E. K. II überreicht und ihm herzlich gratuliert. Sein Kommandant (links), der schon lange das E. K. I und spanische Auszeichnungen trägt, freut sich mit

28 Am Abend hält ein ungeheurer Frieden an! Im U-Bootheim hat sich die ganze Besatzung versammelt. Es gibt besonders gut zu essen und zu trinken. Lieder werden gesungen und selbst improvisierte „Kabarett" der Kameraden wird mit Pfeifen und Handeklatschen be...

29 Und nach ein schöner Lohn für die lange Feindfahrt: Urlaub! Der Obermaschinist der E-Maschine der Signalgast und der Obersteuermann im Urlaubszug. Andere Kameraden sitzen noch ein Teil der Besatzung arbeitet am Boot. Es kommt dran, wenn diese Urlauber zurück...

74

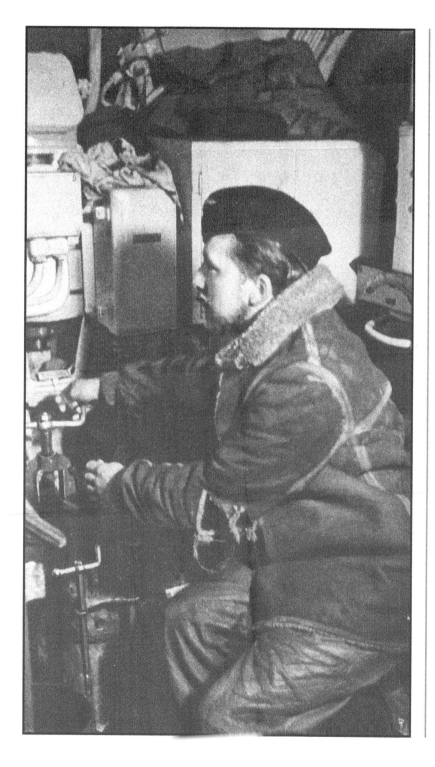

Conditions inside the U-boats were unpleasant at best. The extremes of which varied from unbearable heat running on the Jumbos in tropical waters to freezing cold in the arctic on diesels where sheepskin coats had to be worn even inside the craft.

promising. Its captain, however, had other ideas.

'We set off towards the ship at full speed on the surface and once it got dark we dived, and from a short distance away, discharged a torpedo. But the captain of the ship was so crafty, that when he saw the wake of torpedo - the torpedo runs through the water and the propeller creates a wake, a ripple - he stopped immediately. The torpedo ran past, and as soon as the torpedo had gone past he gave full speed ahead and sailed on. He escaped and we lost our torpedo.'

The U-boats were nonetheless capable of doing extraordinary damage. One convoy ship, the Penelope Barker, struck by two torpedoes from a German submarine, had its 20mm guns blown out of their mountings, its stack knocked down, its bridge partially destroyed and eleven of its crew killed. The Penelope Barker sank in ten minutes together with her cargo of tanks, locomotives and cars.

At home in Germany, exploits like these made Reiners, Karsties and other U-boat men into national celebrities on a par with the

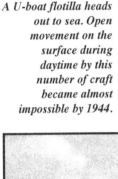

A U-boat flotilla heads out to sea. Open movement on the surface during daytime by this number of craft became almost impossible by 1944.

famous Luftwaffe aces, but Clausdieter Oelschlagel knew that there were shortfalls in the conduct of the struggle that resulted in heavy losses of German submarines and aircraft.

'We made several trips in northern waters, mostly in the Kola inlet in the estuary to the Barents Sea near Murmansk. Initially we didn't have much success in hitting the convoys at sea because our greatest failure was the lack of reconnaissance aeroplanes. We didn't have enough planes at sea to report sightings of convoys in time. The men who were in action in the planes up there, you couldn't envy them. They flew the BV 138, a tri-engine sea-plane, which was relatively slow. If they came across a convoy, mostly with just an auxiliary aircraft carrier as an escort, they were shot down in seconds. That was all badly managed.'

To cut down on losses and improve prospects of success, the Germans devised a new tactic. Its success was limited.

'We knew in advance when an Allied convoy left harbour, in northern Scotland or Iceland. Rather than harry the ships on the way, all our available U-boats were stationed close to Murmansk on the premise that we'd have a better chance if we attacked the convoy as it neared the port. The first time, it worked very well, but the Allies soon cottoned on to what we were doing. The second time, they knew where our U-boats were going to be up to eight days before a convoy set sail. So they lay in wait for us and let us have it. It was depth charges here, depth charges there, depth charges everywhere. It ruined our nerves considerably.

'We had to dive for our own safety and wait for the convoy underwater. What we did was this: we lay on the sand 200 metres down until the convoy sailed by. Then we surfaced and attacked. I was on the U968 and even in those difficult times, we managed to bag a few kills - we sank four or five merchant ships on one occasion.'

Despite the difficulties and the shortfalls, the U-boats and the Luftwaffe managed to make the Murmansk run a veritable gauntlet for the Allied convoys. After June 1941, the Germans sank more than one-fifth of all the supplies sent to Murmansk by convoy. These losses were so severe that the British decided to reduce the Germans'

> "WE LAY ON THE SAND 200 METRES DOWN UNTIL THE CONVOY SAILED BY. THEN WE SURFACED AND ATTACKED."
> CLAUSDIETER OELSCHLAGEL

chances by restricting the convoys to the winter months when the extended nights gave the merchantmen extra cover. In July 1942, however, the rule was broken, with dramatic results.

Early that month, convoy PQ-17, comprising thirty-five ships with a close escort of six destroyers, four corvettes and two anti-aircraft ships, sailed from Iceland bound for north Norway and Murmansk. Distant cover was provided by the British Home Fleet and two ships of the US Navy. The U-boats were waiting and on 4th July, when PQ-17 had already passed north of Bear Island, they fell on the convoy, accompanied by strong Luftwaffe air cover. Their efforts scored minimal success, but then the scenario was abruptly altered. It was reported by Allied air reconnaissance that the battleship Tirpitz, the heavy cruiser Admiral Hipper, the pocket battleship

A chilling image taken through the periscope shows the prey from the perspective of a U-boat captain. Once fixed in this frame the ship's remaining time could be numbered in minutes.

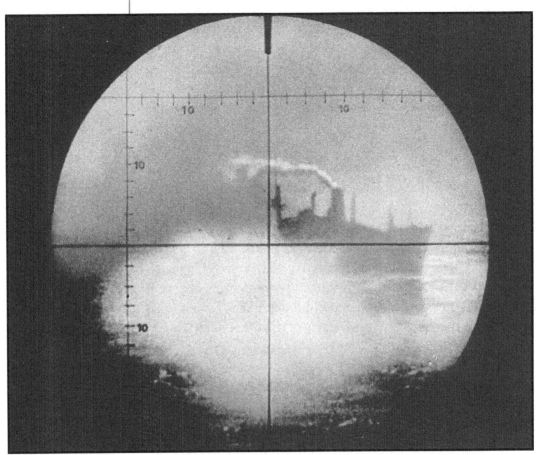

Admiral Scheer and the armoured ship Lützow were heading towards the vicinity of the convoy and would reach the area on the night of 4th/5th July.

The German reason for the presence of these ships in northern waters was the defence of occupied Norway against Allied attack. This was something neither the British nor the Americans fully realised: to them, Tirpitz and the rest were commerce raiders out to add more kills to their already daunting record. From this point of view, their presence close to Convoy PQ-17 made for a first-class emergency and the British and Americans reacted accordingly. Convoy PQ-17 was ordered to scatter on the premise that siting the ships over a wider area would give them some protection. The covering force of cruisers and the six destroyers of the close escort was then ordered to depart and confront the big German surface ships.

It was a disastrous decision. Far from protecting the convoy, it made the task easier for U-boat and Luftwaffe attack and facilitated its destruction. The Germans homed in and only eleven ships of PQ-17 managed to reach their destination. The other twenty-four were all sunk by U-boats and torpedo bombers.

The tragedy of convoy PQ-17 did not end there. It transpired that the reconnaissance report was wrong. The big German ships were still at anchor in Norway, at Altjenfjord until 5th July and though they left port, they returned a few hours later when it transpired that the U boats and the Luftwaffe were quite capable of destroying the ill-fated convoy on their own. Further havoc was wrought upon the surviors of the convoy on the return journey and a further three ships went to the bottom. For a while the Arctic convoys were halted while the allies considered their options. This short interuption gave the Germans one of their few genuine tactical victories of the U-boat war.

THE MEDITERRANEAN

All the same, this spectacular German success in the Arctic was not an accurate guide to the overall situation in which the U-boats found themselves in mid-1942. By then, the U-boats were becoming seriously overstretched in their efforts to patrol three operational zones, the Arctic, the Atlantic and the Mediterranean.

Werner Karsties had already discovered the problem of operating in the Mediterranean, where the Royal Navy and the Royal Air Force were rampant. At stake was the survival of the small, but vital island of Malta which provided bases for the British to patrol the Mediterranean sea routes and protect their forces in Egypt. The Germans also had an important interest: to prevent the British from disrupting the supply lines to the Afrika Korps in North Africa.

German U-boats, Karsties' own craft among them, had been redirected to the Mediterranean after only three months in the Arctic, in September 1941.

'When we were up in the Polar Sea, we were ordered to Gibraltar because a large convoy had been reported, sailing from England to Gibraltar. We lay submerged for two days, surfacing at night to get air, observing the traffic around Gibraltar and waiting for the most suitable moment to get through. Afterwards, getting past Gibraltar proved amazingly difficult. The water currents are completely different whichever way you're going - in, out or out, in. We managed to sail through the Straits of Gibraltar eventually, though we had to do it on the surface. Then we took the boat down to a certain, let's call it 'swimming depth', because the searchlights from Ceuta which was on the Moroccan shore and from Gibraltar on the opposite side, shone just above the tower of the U-Boat. The crew on deck had to duck their heads so that they didn't get caught in the searchlights from both sides. Once we had got through the narrowest part of the Straits, we were lucky enough to be able to dive underneath a fishing fleet and we travelled through most of the Mediterranean under water and landed at Messina. I thought that was my worst experience of the entire war, but I didn't know what was going to happen.

In the Mediterranean, I was the closest I ever came to death. We were attacked in broad daylight by a plane which came out of the Sun so that we couldn't see it. If you look towards the Sun, you can't see anything else but this brilliant glare. It makes your eyes ache. So, out of the blue, or so it seemed, the bombs began to fall. Another aircraft joined in, and we managed to shoot down one of them even though our gun jammed.

Then the second plane fired flares into the air and that lit up the whole area like fireworks night. It was a signal and a destroyer answered it. Fortunately, we managed to dive before we were hit, but we had to stay down at a depth of 200 metres for a full twenty four hours. We didn't dare surface and while we were submerged we were attacked with more than a hundred depth charges. There was a sound like someone was repeatedly striking a small hammer against the metal boat and that told us that the enemy was searching for us by sonar. If there are two destroyers or warships or whatever, and the sonar sounds cross one another, their target is supposed to be at the point where they cross. Now they knew where we were, they kept on

Werner Karsties, who joined the German Navy as a 19 year old volunteer in 1940, rising to the rank of first mate by the end of the war.

raking us with more and more depth charges.

The depth charges were mostly thrown over the stern. We knew that because we could actually hear them being rolled over the deck. There was a pause and then 'Smack!', you could hear them hitting the water. There was a hissing noise and we waited for the bang. Depending on how big the explosion was, you could calculate the sort of damage it was going to do. Fortunately, the depth we were at saved us. The explosive power of depth charges was reduced because of the increased water pressure. So, we managed to escape but I've no doubt that death came very close that day.'

The sea war in the Mediterranean in 1942 was just as ferocious as the action on the Murmansk run. Eighty-one British vessels were sunk and the U-boats accounted for seventy-eight of them. One of their kills was the prestigious aircraft carrier HMS Ark Royal, which was sunk by the U81 on 14th November 1941. The Barham was torpedoed by the U331 eleven days later.

Despite their successes, though, the overall cost to the Germans of the war in the Mediterranean was very high, 38 U-boats were destroyed, most went down with all hands and the number of submarines lost was on the rise. This was no temporary setback. The U-boat crews had given the name 'The happy time' to the halcyon days they had enjoyed in the first years of the War, but now, it was coming to an end.

THE TIDE TURNS

In war, new defences have always been countered by even newer weapons, and vice versa. This was certainly the case in the Second World War at sea and was one of the main reasons why advantage and disadvantage could be claimed to each side in turn during the first four years. Of all the operational theatres, the boost war gives to science and innovation was at its most apparent here and it was when the Allies gained the upper hand both technologically and strategically that the 'Happy Time' between 1939 and 1943 began to turn to days of failure for the U-boats.

The early British and other Allied losses and the vulnerability of the first transatlantic convoys led to a strategic rethink which centralised the routing of the ships, dispersed them over a wide area and strengthened the force of the escorts which protected them against German U-boat and other assaults.

Apart from making attack more difficult, the new Allied strategy made the convoys much harder to find. To counter this, though, the Germans vastly increased their submarine numbers. After 1941, as many as twenty finished U-boats were coming off the slips every month. Helmut Benzing worked on U-boat construction, which was predicated on speed and a high turn-out.

'The U-boats were built in slices, pieces. These were brought in on small ships and in the shipyard, they were set one on top of the other, then they were pressurised and welded together. I suppose you could say they were put together like tin cans. We worked day and night and could launch one U-boat every ten days. It was an ongoing production line, a system building process. Everyone had his own job. Where I worked, we built the flooding rods which allowed the flaps to be opened to let the air out and let the water in

Hamburg-born Helmut Benzing. "I built the U-Boats - I didn't want to sail in them". This picture was taken in 1943.

A picture of Helmut Benzing taken in 1950, upon his release as POW. "We worked day and night and could launch one U-boat every ten days."

The constant watch system meant that there were less bunks than crew. As one man rose for duty another would occupy the still warm bunk. The only solution to the highly demanding job of running the U-boat.

when the submarine had to dive. The rods ran the entire length of the boat up into the command centre and from there, they were opened or closed. I built those, as well as parts of the diesel engines.

It all happened quite quickly. When we'd got a boat ready, the sailors arrived and took it over. It went straight into dock, was tested, sent on trial and then out they went to war.'

The Germans also modified their own strategy and the practice of making individual surface attacks on convoys gave way to the 'wolfpack' technique. This required accurate intelligence and patient reconnaissance, in which the long-range Focke Wulf FW 200 patrol aircraft prowled the Atlantic looking for likely prey.

Prior information enabled the U-boats to reach and patrol areas where convoys were expected well in advance. Once contact was made, there was no immediate attack. Instead, the U-boats shadowed the convoy and signalled other submarines to come and join in the chase. Hunting in packs proved much more effective, and fruitful, than the lone forays typical of the early period in the War and as the U-boats extended their range right across the Atlantic, the Allies had to take even more measures to protect their convoys.

Early on, escorts had been provided for convoys only in the Western Approaches to England. This covered the area south of Ireland, the southern part of the Irish Sea and the western section of the English Channel. The new wide-ranging area of U-boat operations required a greater span of protection, and escorts had to be provided for the whole of the transatlantic passage.

As a result, U-boats began to avoid America and scour the open ocean for easier pickings. Even then, they had to be very careful not to be detected by their prey. Werner Karsties remembers the precautions that had to be taken now that Allied expertise made it that much easier to locate an attacker.

'If a large convoy had been reported, then several U-Boats that were nearby would be ordered to the area. If they were a long distance away, close to America, then it wasn't worth it, but those who were on operations nearby were instructed over the radio that a convoy was at such and such a position and ordered to go there straight away. But there was very little radio contact between U-boats during an operation. That would have enabled the enemy to detect them. They could discover through the radio signal alone, that a U-Boat was sending radio messages, and that 'something' was in the vicinity. Then the people on deck searched even more carefully for German ships and the tops of U-Boat periscopes.'

The new Allied systems certainly provided fewer opportunities for the Germans on the notoriously difficult Murmansk run to northern

"I SUPPOSE YOU COULD SAY THEY WERE PUT TOGETHER LIKE TIN CANS. WE WORKED DAY AND NIGHT AND COULD LAUNCH ONE U-BOAT EVERY TEN DAYS.'"

HELMUT BENZING

Russia, where the destroyer escorts became more and more adept at keeping the U-boats away. Heinrich Schmidt was serving in one of the submarines which attempted to break the defensive ring.

'From 1943 on, we sailed into battle against the convoys, the large convoys that sailed to Murmansk. But they were all well protected by destroyers and U-Boats couldn't get close and were forced away, so we usually came away empty-handed.'

Wherever they were hunting the convoys now, the U-boats faced problems and the problems went on increasing. The Allies made major breakthroughs to claim the upper hand by means of advanced technology. The British introduced the high frequency direction finder of HF/DF, which allowed escort ships to get accurate locations for the U-boats from their radio signals. Usually called 'Huff Duff', the apparatus was extensively used from the autumn of 1941 and could rapidly obtain a bearing even from a brief signal. Huff-Duff remained a secret from the Germans throughout the War and it was a great success, especially in the Atlantic.

So was another innovation introduced in 1941, radar, which had been such a vital factor in the defeat of the Luftwaffe in the Battle of Britain the previous year. During 1941, the mastheads of British destroyers became festooned with radar scanners and these forced more and more U-boats to operate underwater. This meant that their effectiveness was significantly decreased and radar also gave Allied ships the advantage of more accurate navigation in areas of sea fog or limited visibility, both day and night.

At the same time, the lives of U-boat crews were being threatened even more by the introduction of airborne depth bombs. Patrol aircraft were equipped with underwater bombs and search radar, together with high-intensity searchlights for use at night. All this enabled submarines to be detected on the surface at a considerable distance from both aircraft and ships. The 'wolfpack' technique of U-boat attack was now at a disadvantage, since radar and 'Huff

Duff' on board convoy escort vessels provided very effective defence against surfaced wolfpack submarines.

Like the Germans, the Allies instituted a rapid shipbuilding programme which not only aimed to produce cargo vessels faster than the U-boats could sink them, but included increased numbers of antisubmarine patrol and escort vessels chief among them the highly effective Corvette. These excellent vessels were equipped with new weapons, such as the Hedgehog and Squid missiles which were thrown ahead of the ship. The Squid, which had a range of about 300 yards, was a depth-charge projector, developed by the Royal Navy, which consisted of a three-barrelled mortar. It was controlled from the ASDIC sound range recorder and fired a depth charge with fins. The Squid's fuse was set automatically by information from the ASDIC depth-prediction gear.

The Hedgehog, which was more complex, involved firing twenty-four 7.2 inch depth charges in a pattern ahead of the stern. The charges operated on a symbiotic system. They did not explode automatically, only when one or more of them struck a U-boat. This

U154 and U564 involved in a mid Atlantic resupply operation. Speed was of the essence in these operations as the sudden appearance of an Allied aircraft spelled doom for both U-boats.

The daily routine of checking the electric cells took place in the cramped, claustrophobic space under the deck by a crew member on a sliding trolley.

was the signal for the remaining charges to blow up in their turn. This method took into account the requirements of the ship's sonar so that it would not be blanked out by random explosions but could hang on to its sound contact with the submarine. Charges were also thrown from the side and the stern of the attacking Allied ship.

The need for sonar devices for listening, echo ranging and locating submarines was grimly underlined in July 1942, when U-boats sank one hundred and forty ships in the Atlantic. Sonar had been developed long before the War began, but now it became much more sophisticated to enable it to calculate the depth of submarines lurking underwater, detect the presence of incoming torpedoes and decide accurate ranges and bearings and the timing for firing weapons. Heinrich Schmidt remembers what it was like to be underwater, knowing that the sonar was looking for a U-boat and that an attack was sure to follow.

'You know what's going to happen when you hear the sonar coming closer and closer. Then, it finds you and you have to prepare yourself. You can hear the sound of propellers and depth charges. They make eerie noises. The lights go out and parts of the engine shut off. Only someone who has been on a U-boat can describe the feeling. It's sad, a bitter noise, the noise of propellers everywhere above you and you can get terribly anxious. Are they going to drop depth charges or not? You don't know until it happens.'

The Allies took some time to bring their new technological innovations into play. In the interim, there were still insufficient numbers of long range patrol planes based in Britain and America and the wolfpacks, some of them very large, was still able to overcome the convoy escorts. This situation continued even after Adolf Hitler declared war on the Americans and Admiral Donitz

> "IT WAS ONLY THEN THAT WE REALISED THE WAR WAS OVER. IT HAD FINISHED TWO DAYS EARLIER."
> **WERNER VOIGTLANDER**

June 6th 1942: Heinrich Schmidt receives the German Cross.

Plotting the ship's course was a relatively straight forward procedure on the surface but it became incredibly difficult once submerged.

responded by launching an immediate all-out attack on US merchant shipping. He had only five U-boats to spare for this new war, but for six months, until June 1942, they made a killing ground of the American east coast, sinking five hundred vessels. It was as if the 'happy time' had suddenly returned, and U-boat crews made the most of it.

Claus Ohrt of U595 was one U-boat crew member who saw action on the eastern seaboard of America and Canada.

'Once we sank an ammunition ship, it blew up, and from inside we heard the metal fragments banging against the side of the boat.

When we surfaced, an axe on the boat had got stuck, so we made an emblem of this axe; we wore an axe on our caps with the letters USA, that was our emblem.'

At this early stage in their war, American inexperience in all-out warfare at sea was evident from the piecemeal arrangements that masqueraded as convoy protection close to American shores. The Americans learned very quickly, however. They adopted a policy of interlocking coastal convoys and continuous air patrols that made life much more difficult for the U-boats. Caribbean and American coastal waters were considerably safer for convoys after that, and the run of German successes came to an end.

By the latter part of 1942, the Germans had become wary but Claus Ohrt, who served on the U595, remembers that playing safe was not always to their advantage.

'We located a convoy up in the St Laurence stream in Canada. We had to obtain radio permission for an attack, from the High Command of the Wehrmacht. We wanted to start sinking ships, but all we were allowed to do was keep the convoy in sight at a

The Hedgehog was a ferocious addition to the war against the U-boat. The pattern of depth charges landing simultaneously seriously enhanced the possibility of a successful kill.

distance of about ten nautical miles. We were told to report locations continuously, together with numbers of the ships and so on, and had to continuously report locations, where we were, numbers of ships and so on. So we kept on reporting 'Now it's sailing in this direction, now in that direction, taking southerly course or northerly course.' We sent in the report and the High Command tried to order other boats in to intercept and destroy the convoy.

'It took a lot of time, and I think we hung around so long that we were detected. The people in the convoy knew exactly what we were there for, and that we were reporting back on their movements. So, during the night of 16-17 August, we had 250 depth charges dropped on us. Afterwards, we managed to return to Brest. The deep water rudder and everything else were damaged, repairs and maintenance took fourteen days. It happened at other times, too. Every time we shadowed a convoy and reported its movements, we got a terrible thrashing.'

Two weeks was not a long time for repairs. U-boats suffering this sort of onslaught, or simply breaking down, could be out of action

A rare photograph captures the death of a U-boat. The picture was taken from the aircraft that sunk the vessel.

for up to four weeks, and that was if the damage was not too serious. Herbert Lange remembers that 'there was always something wrong with the engines or something else on board.'

'A damaged or defective U-boat was immediately taken to the shipyard. Damage lists were prepared about faults or the repairs we'd been able to make ourselves and we did this while we were still at sea. Once the shipyard had seen to the repair, there was a trial run, and it always took at least four weeks until the boat was ready to put to sea again. It was more if the damage was serious.

Even then, we couldn't always go out on another operation straight away. Very often, the trial run out of the shipyard revealed that something or other was still wrong.

'We had our boat repaired in the shipyard at La Spezia and the Italians gave us a completion date soon after we'd sailed in. We knew the Italians were supposed to be shoddy, careless workers, so we said: "Ha, ha! The Italians take twice as long!' But we were wrong. They were bang on time, the boat was back in top condition, exactly as they had said it would be. Afterwards, our crew didn't need to pick up a spanner when they were out at sea, the boat was in absolutely top condition.'

However, after 1943, four weeks for repairs or even two became a luxury for the U-boats. While they were laid up in dock, other boats that were, as yet, unscathed had to carry the extra strain. Extra work meant more time spent at sea and wider sweeps while there. To handle this situation, the Germans set up a system for maintenance and supply at sea. Large ocean-going Type IX U-boats were converted into supply vessels which acquired the nickname of 'milch cows'. They were able to refuel, rearm and even repair submarines at sea. By this means, the U-boats acquired valuable extra operating time and greater efficiency, but it could be a perilous operation nonetheless. Herbert Lange was on board his U-boat when it was attacked.

'We were caught by English planes that dropped bombs and rockets onto us. One rocket shot through the tower, killing the Duty Officer and twelve men altogether, instantly. Meanwhile the boat was on fire, in the control room. The rocket had hit the oil-pressure gauge equipment which contained about a ton of oil; it ran out and set off a huge blaze, although the central protection walls were closed quite quickly to prevent the fire burning itself out in there. We had twenty live torpedoes on board. The might have started to burn and blow up, but fortunately we got away with it!'

A U-boat attacked on the surface by an Allied aircraft meant a special drill if the wounded were to be saved. Clausdieter Oelschlagel describes what happened.

'During one attack on our boat, we had one man killed and 7 injured from the Flak gunners. The rest of us had to drop them down the open hatch Whoomp! onto a large carpet or woollen mat. They fell down onto that and were rolled out of the way. Then those of us who were all right jumped down after them. You have to be able to do it extremely well, to jump in one after the other, because if a life jacket or a leather jacket got snagged on the way down, it could have had dire consequences. Our commander trained us specially to escape in this way. We practised for the whole day in the Ovik fjord near Narvik, up and down, up and down again and again so that we were fit for the job at sea.'

Herr Orht's U-boat had a remarkable escape, due to the mysterious absence of Allied aircraft in an area - the Bay of Biscay - where they were usually numerous.

'We had to dive because the deep water rudders were broken, we were stuck and only able to carry out a half-dive by going into reverse when we wanted to submerge. It was likely to take us twenty minutes to get from the surface down to the bottom. Nonetheless - and I haven't been able to understand it to this very day - we managed to sail through the Bay of Biscay into Brest without interference. We were in a really bad state, not being able to dive properly. Yet, we weren't attacked by planes, English planes, we weren't attacked by destroyers or corvettes. That was normally a daily occurrence when a U-boat tried to reach harbour at Brest. We just sailed right through.'

Kurt Wehling's last trip came to an abrupt end after his U-boat was forced to the surface.

'Depth charges didn't always explode on the boat one hundred percent of the time. They were spread about because the Allied ships didn't know exactly where our boat was. The depth charges were fired over the sides of the ships and spread around. If they exploded close to the boat then they caused damage - the valves opened and water came in, that's what it was like. On the last trip we had to surface because the first depth charges were dropped quite close by and ripped the boat open. We weren't sunk by depth charges but by the ship's artillery, they got us.'

On 8 November 1942, the Americans entered the war on land when they participated in Operation Torch, the Allied landings in North Africa. The U595 was in the Mediterranean with orders to 'prevent the landings'. Claus Ohrt was on board.

'Our orders were to 'prevent the Allied landings in Africa'. That's how it was phrased, anyway. We were supposed to close off the harbour entrance at Oran. Around 10 November, we sank a ship, not a big one, only five or six thousand tonnes, and an Allied transport ship or something like that. We knew the enemy was using radar against us all the time. We could hear it. It sounded like peas being thrown out in a saucepan, but we weren't too bothered about that. We were young, you see, so we didn't take it too seriously. Then, on 14

A U-boat leaving the port of Kiel for another operational patrol in the early war years.

November, we got the order from Admiral Donitz not to sail on the surface in the Mediterranean during the day. We knew the reason, for we no longer had air cover, in fact as we discovered later, we no longer had a proper airforce. We set off shortly before 0800 hours, just as I was about to relieve the watch, and there was this unbelievable crash. The galley flap flew open, a bomb had exploded on top of it, the galley flap opened, and the alarm bell went off simultaneously. We saw this huge hole and through that, we could see the sky. One of my shipmates - quite a tall fellow - grabbed hold of me and lifted me up. I got hold of the ring and then bang, the galley flap was shut tight again. There were four catches, and it slammed closed over them but then water began to leak through it. We tried to twist it but we couldn't make it close down tight properly. Fortunately, it stayed closed because the water pressure held it down.'

The U595 dived, but it was too badly damaged to remain for long below the surface.

'We dived down and the pressure gauge in the engine room told us that we had dropped over 250 metres. That was when water broke into the electric engine room. We were ordered to go to the front of the boat, then air was pumped in and we resurfaced. The whole episode lasted about five minutes, including diving and resurfacing. The starboard diesel was water-logged, but the port side diesel was all right and started up at once. We moved off straight away, but immediately we were attacked from the air. All we could do now was defend ourselves and hope to survive. We were told to head for Spain, but the damage to the boat was too great for that and we were ordered to sail instead towards the African coast. We had a 2cm flak gun fixed on the deck and set up two machine guns which had recently been welded to the boat in the marine base at Brest. We were also carrying shells to use against armoured planes.

'A little later, we managed to get the starboard engine running again and we sailed towards Africa. Even though it was dangerous to be there, we were so exposed, many of tried to stay on deck because we knew that if the boat sank, we had the best chance of survival. If we'd be down below, our chances wouldn't have been too good.'

Being on deck also gave Ohrt a grandstand view of the opposition they were facing.

'On deck, we saw planes all around us, at least nine of them. Gerhard Horn, who was manning the flak gun, was a trained artillery man and he let the enemy planes get close, up to about 250 metres, before he began to fire. The rest of us packed the cartridges for the gun so that he wouldn't run out of ammunition. Although there were so many aircraft, they didn't come into the attack in groups. They always attacked one at a time, so it was that much easier to see them off.

What I didn't find out until after the War, when I met two of the pilots, was that they were scared stiff of our armament. They said they had been much more scared than we were, because they didn't know what we were hitting them with. That's why they stopped attacking us and so allowed our boat to sail on towards Africa. But we were in a terrible state. The back of the boat sank, water had broken into the electric engines, and the boat became heavier and heavier at the stern. It went up at the front and down at the back and suddenly we only had eight or ten metres of water beneath the keel.

'The order came 'All men overboard!', and then out we went, and then we sank the boat. When we were in the water - we were defenceless, of course - a plane came over and shot at us. But it only made one run, thank goodness. No one was seriously hurt except one man, Walter Holdorf, who was shot through the thigh.'

Ohrt and the rest of the crew of U595 had not yet finished their adventures. Onshore, on the African coast, they were twice attacked, once from the air, on the other occasion from the sea.

'We managed to get ashore and you won't believe this when I tell you. Another aircraft flew over and dropped leaflets on us. The pilot said that if we didn't stay where we were, then he would fire at us. Well, we ran off, he returned and opened fire but we had all hidden ourselves behind stones and no one was hit. He flew off after that. The next thing we knew, there was a destroyer offshore bombarding us with artillery. We were lucky again, because only one salvo was fired, it didn't hit anything or anyone, and then they stopped.

'Because Holdorf was injured, we signalled the destroyer to send a boat to fetch him on board. Holdorf became a prisoner, but at least he was well looked after and his injuries tended. The rest

In the early years of the war the Luftwaffe were able to support the activities of the U-boats. This shot was taken from the observation window of a Heinkel III.

of us marched off in the direction of Oran. We met a French policeman and asked him if he could help us, we wanted to get dry and all that, and he said that we could spend the night in the school. But you know how it goes, the English got to hear about us and radioed the Americans to say that a German U-Boat crew had landed, go get them. Four American tanks rolled up and took us prisoner, the only U-Boat crew to be captured by tanks. We were taken to Oran, where we were presented to the population as a German U-Boat crew, they stood us up in the town square and told everyone that we were criminals. Well, that's how they regarded us. After that, we were taken to the citadel and, if you didn't already have lice or fleas, then you caught them there from the bed clothes.'

On his voyage to captivity in America, Ohrt saw for the first time the immense power of the Allies at sea.

'That same night we were sent on board a ship called the Brazil, a 20,000 tonner, where we were stowed in the engine room, and

Krupp's yard was charged with the responsibility of the crash building programme which resulted in the rapid expansion of the U-boat fleet.

taken off to America. After three days were we allowed on deck for the first time. I've never seen anything in my entire life like that, such equipment. An aircraft carrier, six destroyers with smaller ships in attendance, even a cruiser I think. The convoy consisted of perhaps fourteen ships, all sailing towards America.'

Being forced to surface, like Ohrt's submarine, naturally put the vessel in much greater danger of being attacked. The severe damage and ultimate sinking of the U595 proved what happened when a craft was obliged to abandon the comparative safety of the underwater depths. To enable U-boats to remain submerged for longer at a time when air and surface ship radar were already making life very difficult for them, the Germans introduced the snorkel, a hollow retractable mast which contained tubes for fresh air intake and for the engine exhaust.

Heinz Reiners' father-in-law helped to design the snorkel, which was fitted to the U-boats after 1944. As an experienced submariner himself, Reiners' was well aware of the advantages of the snorkel, but also some of the disadvantages.

'The air inside a U-boat was dreadful, so when my father-in-law helped to design the snorkel, he was doing U-boat crews a great favour. You could unfold the snorkel's long tube and while we stayed submerged, only the top of the snorkel where the air was sucked in was above water. Before this, we'd always had to surface to charge the battery and air the boat, but now we could do it underwater. We could keep moving, too while we were doing it. But the snorkel didn't work so well if the water was choppy and there were waves on the surface. The check-valve would snap closed and then it sucked diesel fumes from the engine room resulting in negative pressure. In the galley if the cook, the 'Smut' as we called him, was hanging over his pots they flew up in to the air. It drove you mad, the different pressures when the snorkel was out.'

When the snorkel was first introduced, Allied radar was not yet advanced enough to pick up the end of the mast as it poked up above the surface. Later radars had this capability, however, so that the snorkel became yet another method by which U-boats could be detected and attacked. Reiners recalls being targeted.

'You always knew when the sonar was after you. The sound comes closer and closer and then it found you and you knew what was going to happen next. We had to prepare ourselves. We could hear the sound of ships' propellers approaching and the sound of the depth charges. Depth charges and destroyer make eerie noises, the lights go out and parts of the engine too. Only someone who's been on a U-boat can describe the feeling. It is a bitter and sad noise when the destroyers and depth charges are coming, the noise of the propellers everywhere above you, they can get you very, very anxious...'

Werner Ziemer, too, found the propellers noises thoroughly unnerving.

'They sounded like 'Sshh-sshh. You can hear each blade slicing through the water. Nowadays the propellers have multiple blades, in those days they only had three. You could also hear the sonar echoing inside the boat. It went tick tick tick tick tick — tick tick tick. It was unnerving, really unnerving.'

Increased Allied vigilance and more success in destroying U-boats had a knock-on effect on the U-boat war. Werner Karsties observes how the U-boats were denied time to update their equipment in harbour.

'Naval technology advanced a great deal during the course of the War, not only on the German side but also in England. The English ships were faster, more accurate and could find us much more easily than they could in the early year. As a result, our losses increased and those U-boats which survived had to do more work than before. We were continuously in action at the front. Boats could only be improved when they returned from operations against the enemy. The commanders were supposed to report what they had experienced through being intercepted by the enemy, and told the technicians on land what had to be done. But after 1943, there just wasn't enough time for this to be done properly.'

U-boat crews had to be careful, too, how the hatch was closed before diving. Herr Voigtlander explains the problems this caused when, later on, the U-boat had to surface.

> "YOU COULD ALSO HEAR THE SONAR ECHOING INSIDE THE BOAT. IT WENT TICK TICK TICK TICK TICK - TICK TICK TICK. IT WAS UNNERVING, REALLY UNNERVING."
> WERNER ZIEMER

'You can't get the tower hatch open after surfacing until you have established pressure equalisation between the air outside and the air inside. It used to happen that if someone fastened the tower hatch too tightly when they dived, they couldn't open it again once they were on the surface. Even when the pressures were equalised, you could do what you liked, the rubber ring was so tightly sealed that they couldn't get it open again! The only thing to do was to dive again straight away so that you could get some pressure on it and loosen it before resurfacing. After that, you could open it.

'Equalisation of pressure causes steam, anything that is wet suddenly evaporates into steam and the whole boat is filled with mist, sometimes a lot sometimes less depending on the position. The ventilation had to be turned on immediately. We really couldn't afford mistakes like this when there might be Allied aircraft prowling around ready to drop bombs on us while we were more occupied with opening the hatch than firing back at them.'

Constant vigilance was a must for U-boats which could be attacked at any moment and in the later part of the War, Werner von Voigtlander remembers, a double watch system was introduced.

'Towards the end, on the Type XXI, U-boats, the previous triple-shift system - eight hours on watch at a time - was abandoned and the double watch system replaced it. On the Type XXI we had two watch periods, which weren't that dramatic, because for the most part the boat travelled under water. When we were submerged, two men were at the deep sea rudder, one on the rudder working the levers, and once the submerged boat had been set on course by the Chief Engineer, after the diving procedure, then the duty officer took over the responsibility and we continued to travel under water. He sat in the control room and made sure that nothing happened whilst the others slept and two or three men looked after the engines. Otherwise we were on watch every 4 hours, and believe me, when we were on the surface, there wasn't much sleep to be had. We had to reckon the enemy could appear and attack us at any time.'

In this tense situation, U-boat crews had to protect themselves in any way they could, even if it meant attacking civilian targets.

Werner Karsties' U-boat was in the eastern Mediterranean, close to the coast of Palestine, when the fishing boats common in the area came under suspicion.

'During the last days of my service in the Mediterranean, we sank lots of small fishing boats with the 8-8 gun. They were really harmless fishing boats around Haifa and Jaffa and in the early days of the War - the 'happy time' - we probably wouldn't have touched them. But later, we thought that these boats might pick up something on the radio and we knew they had some very modern equipment, these harmless fishing boats. They could radio to the shore immediately and it wouldn't be long before enemy planes arrived. That was why it was necessary to sink them immediately without bothering to search them or investigate them.'

German anxieties in the latter half of the War were exacerbated by the very punishing casualty rate suffered by the U-boats. In all, around sixty percent of all U-boat personnel were lost during the War and it was not unusual for U-boats to manage only two sorties before they were destroyed. There was a dearth of young officers and battle-hardened crew and many submarines had to put to sea commanded by inexperienced young men in their early 'twenties. Some of the submarines were undermanned and this made them even

A Kreigsmarine review: senior officers accept the salute from the U-boat crews passing in line ahead.

more vulnerable. Several U-boats, and their young crews, were lost on their very first voyage.

Werner Karsties remembers that U-boat commanders had their own solution to the problem of inexperienced crews. It worked for a time, but only for a time.

'Every commander made an effort to keep the core crew, with which he had taken over the boat from the shipyard, with him for as long as possible. This had always been our practice at least until the middle of the War. If a boat was in for repairs, and you knew how long the repairs would take - four, six, eight weeks - a U-boat crew wasn't dispersed. Of course, it was possible that someone or other would be ordered away, someone on another boat in the flotilla would become ill, and then the First Duty Officer or the helmsman would go out with that boat as long as, theoretically, he could get back on his own boat when it was ready.

'The U-boat flotillas used to organise all this between themselves. There was also a flotilla reserve - men on stand-by in La Rochelle, in Bordeaux, or wherever, who were assigned to duty if someone left a boat or became ill. But essentially, the core crew remained together. Later on, though, that was no longer possible because of the losses, which led to men being ordered away to other boats or to NCO training. These NCOs were sent to other boats and were replaced by new men from the U-boat training schools. So commanders could still end up with inexperienced crews.'

The U-boats themselves were not always in the peak of condition and inexpert handling made the situation worse. Werner von Voigtlander was serving on the U415 when a potentially fatal accident occurred.

'Three days after I reported for duty at Kiel, our U-boat suddenly went crashing down to a depth of 250 metres because of a mechanical failure during the dive. I sat on my deep-sea rudder box and thought 'It's not that great on this boat, is it?' The ship was leaking water which dripped down on everyone and nothing worked.

Fortunately, our people managed to get the boat back up again, but

A lucky survivor awaits rescue in the aftermath of the sinking of U172. Although the U-boat crews were extensively trained in survival techniques, the actual chances of survial from a submerged U-boat were vanishingly small.

there were so many mechanical failures because of the 'top deck tubes', as we called them. We found that the water pressure had been so great that it had squashed the reserve torpedoes flat. It was close call at that depth.'

Towards the end of 1943, the U415 was back in action and on Christmas Day, the boat became embroiled with a destroyer.

'The destroyer wanted to ram us and came thundering towards us. We were at periscope depth and had to dive at once. We released an acoustic torpedo from our tube 5, kept right on target and the destroyer was hit and sank. We managed to rescue about four casualties from the destroyer, but it was all very unpleasant. It was Christmas Day, not a day for killing and destruction.'

The U415 returned to Brest to rejoin the First U-Boat Flotilla and then Voigtlander was ordered to retrain for service on the Type XXI U-boats which represented a new concept in U-boat construction.

'The XXIs were welded together in three shipyards; those with the numbers 25 in Hamburg, those with the number 30 in Bremen and those with the number 35 in the east, in Danzig. We were sent to U3001 but it wasn't put into service because it had some very bad technical defects. The Type XXI was the first attempt to make a U-Boat by shoving together, pushing and welding together different parts. The ducts had to fit together and if someone forgot to remove a flange, then nothing worked. Later, when the 02 was put into service, we got quite a few surprises. The 02 was lost because of a breakdown in the harbour at Kiel. We got the propellers tangled in the nets that were designed to catch the torpedoes.

'Ours was the first boat of that type to arrive in Kiel. We went into reverse in front of the bunker so as to be able to sail in slowly, which caused the stern to sink a little and then 'Whoomp!' we got entangled in the thing and the boat was unfit for service. We were towed away by another boat to the docks in Flensburg where they discovered that it was hopeless, it couldn't be repaired quickly.'

The Kriegsmarine had now entered a fatal spiral. Allied shipbuilding was climbing far above Allied losses at sea. On the U-boats, reducing experience and rising losses meant that young greenhorn crews were going to sea in what had almost become a 'turkey shoot'.

Long-range aircraft, such as the British Short Sunderland flying boat and the American Liberator fitted with long-range tanks were able to seek out the U-boats as never before. Surfacing became even more dangerous: the U-boats could come under attack immediately from Allied aircraft patrolling the skies above. However, not surfacing also had its perils. Kurt Wehling was involved in a depth charge attack that forced his U-boat to remain submerged for eight hours. Eventually, despite the dangers, the boat was obliged to surface because the crew was having trouble breathing.

'We were short of air, critically short, in fact. So we had to surface, come what may. We were lucky on that occasion. The enemy was nowhere to be seen, but everyone lay on the floor with respirators, gasping for air through our apparatus. We were able to air the boat, and what a relief that was, I can tell you!'

By mid-1942, the Allies had perfected their compact airborne radar system which enabled them to detect a surfaced submarine several miles away. This gave them the advantage of surprise. U-boat commanders could suddenly find themselves confronted with a heavily armoured aircraft swooping down out of the clouds and flying straight at them on a bombing run. Clausdieter Oelschlagel was on board one U-boat that was attacked in this terrifying fashion.

'The Liberators came tearing down forty or sixty metres above the sea. On 17th July, we were attacked by a Liberator bomber and were lucky enough to hit it on approach. We shot that one down, but two days later, another Liberator arrived. We were taken by surprise, confused, and didn't know whether we should dive or not. We remained on the surface and the Liberator raked us very badly. One

U46 returns to port with a damaged bridge, but the fluttering pennants bring news of fresh sinkings.

man died and seven were injured on the bridge. We managed to dive several hours later, catch our breath and recuperate a bit, and then went staggering off back home.'

By this time, the Allies already had an advantage of which the Germans were unaware. In 1941, the Royal Navy had managed to get hold of the top secret Enigma code book from the crippled German weather ship. All signals to U-boats were coded and could be decoded only by means of this book. It was now a simple matter to crack the German codes, and one of the benefits was that the

Allies were able to identify the positions of the U-boat 'wolf packs'.

The Germans had had the Enigma machine for enciphering radio transmissions for twenty years by this time, and during the Second World War they changed their codes every day. Different branches of their armed forces used different codes, and the Germans came to believe that the system was foolproof. They never realised that French intelligence had helped Polish mathematicians and cryptanalysts build copies of Enigma, which they had handed over to the British and the French before the War began. The capture of the Enigma code book in 1941 was also unknown to them and so was a similar incident that occurred in 1944.

It happened off the Cape Verde Islands, when an Allied force on patrol captured the U505. The submarine's code books were seized intact, enabling naval experts to decipher the German naval codes. Werner Karsties recalls what happened after the Allies got their hands on this invaluable German secret.

'They should have thrown the log book into the sea, those people on the U505 but either they forget or weren't able to. So the Allies got hold of it and then the code machine also fell into their hands. The code machine was used for decoding the radio messages which were not in 'clear'. They were encoded, - A was B or C was E, not as simple as that, of course, but you get the idea - and the code was changed every 24 hours. The message had to be decoded on board the U-boat and then handed to the commander. But the Allies got hold of all this and according to one story I heard, they sent false coded messages ordering U-boats to a certain point and when they got there, they bombed them.'

The breaking of the codes produced an even more dramatic rise in German U-boat losses. In one month - May 1943 - thirty-seven boats were lost. Another thirty-four went down in July. Werner von Voigtlander's craft, the U415, was one of those that managed to escape this massacre, but it was a very close run thing.

'It was 8th May 1943, a day I'll never forget as long as I live. Four-engined planes came down at us from out of the clouds - huge machines. We knew that if enemy aircraft looked the size of

On his return to port, Captain Thurman is interviewed for the everpresent propaganda machine.

mosquitoes on the horizon, then the boat could dive and you were safe. But these planes were big, big, big and we had no chance. In any case, we had orders to remain on the surface and fight them off from there. It may sound strange, but there was good thinking behind it. You see, bombs from the air sink to perhaps five metres below the surface before exploding and if the boat is down at twelve or fifteen metres, then that's it, it's finished. kaput! The depth charges were specially adjusted to explode much deeper - at fifty or sixty metres below the surface. If the U-Boat had dived, the aircraft saw a big whirlpool and they'd take their time and aim. There was no one to disturb them by firing at them, and they dropped their depth charges in this whirlpool. If the U-boat was in the diving phase, and down, let's say, up to eighty metres, with all the hatches open, the catches open, then the depth charge exploded right beside the boat and blew it to smithereens. That caused huge losses, of course, so that's why we were told to stay on the surface. We just had to sit there and take it until the aircraft had finished dropping their bombs or until they had withdrawn to a distance, perhaps in order to make a fresh approach. That gave us time to dive down to a safe depth before they came back, but we had to dive well over eighty metres or they'd get us the second time.

'We didn't have much of a chance, though. On the U415 we had just one weary old 2 cm and they had lots of on board guns, machine guns and heaven knows what. We tried to manoeuvre out of danger. We went right and left at full speed ahead, hard to port, hard to starboard, trying to get out of it. It was useless. All the things they threw at us - bombs, depths charges, all the damage! One of the depth charges exploded right under the stern and the boat practically stood on its head. We closed the tower hatch but it didn't lock. It wasn't hermetically sealed. There's a click-spring to close it from outside; so the hatch was open a way. We were strapped in with our broad belts and the steel straps for stability in the waves and the boat sliced down to about four or five metres. In other words, we were roped onto the bridge and then there were perhaps five or six metres of water above us.

'When the boat tipped up and stood on its head because of the depth charge explosion, our Chief Engineer at once realised what had happened. He could see where the boat was from his depth gauge. He immediately had the water chambers discharged, let pressurised air into the flood tubes and drove the whole thing back up. But for one or two minutes, we had to hold our breath. I saw nothing but green and more green, and spluttered. I thought 'The show is over'. and then, pppffff! Suddenly everything became lighter and we were out. We'd been lucky.'

If the sea was being made dangerous for the U-boats, there was no much more security in dock. Karl Ohrt's submarine was berthed in Hamburg when it got caught up the last raid on the already flattened city in 1943.

'I was on watch at the time. It was a daytime raid and there was no air raid siren to warn us. I heard the bombs falling and I sent the crew members who were still on board on watch duty into the bunkers as fast as possible. I remained on board with one or two others. The bombs fell into the harbour and our diving tanks were badly damaged. We were towed into the bunker at Rohwald, but the damage was so serious, it couldn't be repaired.'

Werner Karsties remembers how U-boats crews being depth-charged received some assurance in their predicament from a fail-safe procedure that could save them even if their ship were lost.

'We could get to the surface from quite far down, from perhaps a depth of about sixty metres. Everyone had a respirator on his life jacket and the control room would be flooded so that the pressure would be equal to the outside water-pressure and the tower hatch could be opened. You then had to open the valve, not too quickly, so that you moved upwards, but slowly. Unfortunately, far too

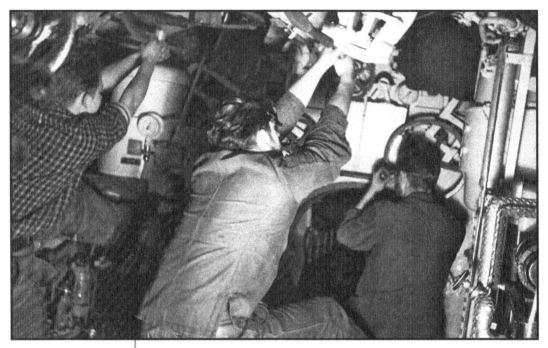

Purging the ballast for a dive required a great deal of physical struggle.

many men panicked, opened up the valve and shot up to the surface. Then they were poisoned by the nitrogen so that blood flowed out of their mouth and nose. No, when escaping from a U-boat, you needed to keep calm. It was a great reassurance for us. We knew that there was a way to get out even if the boat was doomed.'

Kurt Wheling's U-boat was doomed when his U-boat set out for a foray in the Mediterranean and ran into a powerful convoy escort.

'We were in front of a convoy and sank one ship. But immediately afterwards, the first depth charges fell and hit us. The boat had cracks in it and we had to creep away, keeping absolutely quiet inside the boat. There were three destroyers above us, three! They searched and searched and searched with their equipment, Ping-ping-ping-ping, we heard it. The small pinging sounds meant they hadn't found us, but if the ASDIC went 'Ping - P-I-N-G!', when it bounced back, then we were in the soup. Another destroyer sailed up after the first and dropped more depth charges. By this time it was 2000 hours. We crept forward in silence and they kept on searching but somehow we managed to get away with it and they gave up. After another two hours, we had to surface because too much water had leaked into the boat. Once we had surfaced, the duty crew immediately went up into the tower and manned the twin 2cm machine guns. Good thing, too! We had hardly emerged from the water before we were caught in the searchlights of three destroyers. They opened fire immediately with their artillery. The crew on duty on our U-boat answered by opening fire on the searchlights.

'One shell hit us directly in the tower and there was a stench down at the bottom of the tower from the explosion, the stink of dynamite. My role down below was to pass on the commands - they weren't given through a microphone, each command was passed from man to man. The Chief Engineer in the control room suddenly shouted, 'Everybody out', probably because he hadn't received any more orders from the tower. The commander was no longer there because of the direct hit. I stood between the control room and the commander's room and was one of the first four men to get out. I got up on deck, there were searchlights all around us. It was as light as day and the guns on the destroyers were still thundering away. We had one-man rubber dinghies that were distributed all around the boat and in an emergency everyone could grab one, tie it around himself like a little brief case with two cords. I took one and once I was out and in the water, I turned on the little pressurised gas bottle. It went Shhhhhh! and out came the boat. I draped my arm into it and paddled away on my own.

'It was very dark. Each of us had a whistle so that all those who were nearby could gather together. I heard the first whistle but I didn't answer. I thought 'Stay on your own, stay on your own'. Who knows what's going to happen, you've got a one-man rubber dinghy, you can paddle. But it didn't take long before a wave threw someone over, then there were two of us, and in the end there were four of us with two rubber dinghies. The dark was a blessing because after a while, the destroyers returned to their convoy. Then, a searchlight appeared on the horizon, came closer and closer and some English sailors fished us out of the water. They set boats down and I remember there was a big black man - the first

black man I'd ever seen. He was a big, strong fellow. He grabbed hold of us and pulled us out of the water. We were taken back to the destroyer and went on board. We were well treated. They showed us immediately to a room where we could have a shower. Each of us was given a Red-Cross parcel in which there was a pair of pyjamas, toothpaste, socks and shoes, felt slippers that is. We went into another room, and found the table was set with ham, bread, packets of cigarettes and heaven knows what. It was all very welcome.'

German losses were at their highest in the Atlantic, where the only victories they scored were usually pyrrhic victories. In October

The control room of U522 during a depth charge.

1943, for instance, the U-boats sank one escort ship and three merchant ships, but lost twenty-two of their own craft. This was in sharp contrast even to the flawed success of a wolf pack six months earlier when the U-boats attacked Convoy ONS-5, en-route to Newfoundland and sank thirteen merchant vessels for the loss of six submarines.

Ultimately, the cost became too great for the service to bear and Admiral Donitz was belatedly forced to order the complete withdrawal of the U-boats from the north Atlantic. Despite this sensible measure the U-boat war itself was not at an end. On 6th June 1944 the Allies sent the largest amphibious invasion force ever known across the English Channel to land in Normandy on D-Day, 1944, forty-five German U-boats were waiting for them. However, it was to be their last concerted stand, and all but fifteen were destroyed. By this time, the Allies were also wrecking the U-boats at source, in the submarine pens. Werner von Voigtlander was about to sail in a new U-boat when the Allied bombers came over.

'Two days before we were due to sail, there was an air raid and the boat sank, right beside the pier. One of our men was inside, to the rear. Twenty-four hours later, we still hadn't got him out. It just wasn't possible. We tried to pull it up with a tugboat but all the cables tore, we couldn't cut it open because he would have drowned in there. He was quite a young NCO, but he didn't know Morse code. He just kept banging madly on the walls of the boat. But it was no use. He died.'

Despite their desperate situation, the Germans were still introducing new methods of promoting the underwater war. One of their technological innovations was the Type 5 acoustic torpedo which was designed to home in on engine noise. Clausdieter Oelschlagel had a poor opinion of the Type 5, which U-boat crews called Zaunkönig, the wren.

'In my opinion, the Zaunkönigen weren't much good because the convoys soon had a defence against them. The sloops or corvettes would tow a 'rattle' buoy at a distance of about 200 metres behind them. It was a noise-making buoy. That attracted the T5 torpedo and the stupid thing headed towards the sound and exploded there. It was such a simple method they used, but 'Poof!' in a moment a marvellous weapon on which many engineers had worked for years went up in smoke!'

Life aboard the U-boats also encompassed long lonely hours of boredom hunting for targets in what sometimes appeared to be empty oceans.

Krieg Künstlers (war artists) served on board some of the U-boats and presented a unique impression of the Atlantic battles.

U-Boote im Atlantik

This vivid and highly dramatic portrayal of a U-boat action is unrealistic for this late stage of the war. By 1944 U-boat attacks were almost always made from beneath the surface.

Deutsche Unterseeboote, so gab das Oberkommando der Wehrmacht bekannt, griffen nach wochenlanger Pause überraschend in feindlichen Geleitverkehr im Nord-Atlantik an. Es gelang einer U-Boots-Kampfgruppe, einen nach Amerika fahrenden Geleitzug zu erfassen, der ungewöhnlich stark gesichert war. Die Angriffe mußten daher gegen die außerordentlich zahlreichen Geleitzerstörer der Außensicherung geführt werden. Hierbei erzielten die deutschen Unterseeboote einen einmaligen Erfolg. In tagelangen hartnäckigen und erbitterten Kämpfen wurden zwölf feindliche Zerstörer versenkt und drei weitere torpediert. Starker Nebel behinderte die Fortsetzung der Operationen, trotzdem wurden aus dem Geleitzug noch neun Schiffe mit 46 500 BRT. versenkt und zwei weitere torpediert.

PK-Zeichnung
Kriegsberichter
Hans Liska

THE LAST VICTORY

Claus Oelschlagel took part in the last operation undertaken by a German U-boat against a British warship when the sloop Gudel was sunk in Norwegian waters on 29 April 1945.

'We had a report from the First Officer on the Gudel which we were given after the War: apparently 117 men were lost with the ship. That was my last trip and after we had sunk the Gudel we were heavily attacked with depth charges by other destroyers and sloops in the area. Our attack periscope was hit, flooded with water so that we only had the second, the air periscope or 'knee-bend' periscope. That's the one you see in films when the commander stands at the periscope and goes up and down. We called it the 'knee-bend' periscope, whereas the attack periscope was automatic. That was still intact, but had the disadvantage of an enormous head that could easily be seen. On the return trip to Narvik following the 29th April, we spotted another convoy on our starboard side but it was far away, and we were ordered to sail into harbour and not attack any more, just defend ourselves if attacked. We sailed into Haarstad in the Lofoten Islands where there was an important naval office, and on to Narvik.'

On 4th May 1945, five days after Oelschlagel's last U-boat voyage, Admiral Karl Donitz, now German Head of State since Hitler's suicide on 30th April, issued an order for the submarines to cease hostilities. Donitz was highly respected by the U-boat crews and to judge from his final words to them, the feeling was mutual.

'My U-boat men', Donitz told them. 'Six years of warfare lie behind us. You have fought like lions against a crushingly superior force, but you are unbroken in your warlike courage. You are laying down your arms after an heroic fight without equal. In reverence, let us think of the many comrades who have died. Comrades! Maintain your U-boat spirit with which you fought most bravely and

The sinking of U570 by American surface vessels. The phosphorescent trace which the U-boat produced can be clearly seeen even in this daytime shot.

unflinchingly during the long years.'

Since 1939, seven hundred and thirty three U-boats had been lost together with seventy nine Italian submarines. A total of 2,753 Allied ships of 14,557,000 gross tons had been sunk.

Clausdieter Oelschlagel was still in Narvik when Nazi Germany surrendered on 7th May 1945 and remained there for nearly three weeks more.

'We were still in Narvik on 25th May. Our boat was lying in one of the fjords, but no one came. We were then given permission to transfer to Trondheim where the Flotilla was and where we had our belongings. We got as far as the entrance to the fjord at Trondheim where we met a Canadian fleet and they ordered the U-Boats to go to Scotland. Half the crew were taken off there, and the rest of us sailed to Lisholly near Londonderry in Ireland.

'After that, we were all sent to England where we ended up in a tent camp at Butterly. On the way, we officers were locked in the ladies' toilets at Hampton Court Palace - well, it was one way to get a look at a royal palace, I suppose!'

Werner von Voigtlander's war ended in a much more curious fashion. His U-boat was at sea when the surrender of Nazi Germany was announced, but the crew knew nothing about it.

'We were halfway across the 'big pond', heading for America. We didn't know that the war was over because our special longwave radio equipment wasn't working. The reason for that was the capture of the big transmitter near Magdeburg by the Allies. So we were cut off from the world. We didn't surface, we were a full-snorkel boat which meant we could sail for hours under water. Then we started to intercept some strange messages - or at least, we thought they were strange. There was one from a stoker in Wilhelmshaven who was sending greetings to a female naval assistant in Oslo - What a load of rubbish we thought!

'Then the English sent an open radio message, saying that we should deliver our boat to Loch Eribol up in Scotland, hoist the black flag, throw the ammunition overboard and surrender. We thought it was a rotten trick. We weren't going to fall for that, we said. But just the same we suspected something was wrong, we didn't know what, so we decided to sail back to Norway. Three quarters of the way there, when we were heading towards Bergen, it occurred to us that maybe the Russians were there. That was something we didn't want - not under any circumstances! So we changed course again and decided to go home to Germany through the Baltic Sea. It was risky, because we didn't have any mine charts for the Baltic. Then, suddenly, we heard a dreadful noise under the water and our sound detector picked up signs of an entire fleet sailing by. We looked through the periscope and there was an English invasion fleet sailing across to Norway. Cruisers and battle ships one behind the other. We watched them calmly, and submerged a little.

'It was only then that we realised the War was over. It had finished two days earlier, and no one knew our U-boat was in the area. Well, we had twenty-four torpedoes on board, and we could have fired them, one every thirty seconds at a depth of seventy metres. It was a completely new technique which had never been used. But we didn't use it. Instead, we worked our way through the minefields around Scargen and while we were doing that, we were sighted by an English plane. We were in a fix. We thought the plane might bomb us. Our signalling equipment - a small spotlight - was destroyed, so we couldn't report the number of our boat that way. Instead, we had to write our number - 3008 - on the metal deck with some chalk. That seemed to satisfy the English pilot and he flew away.

'Next thing we knew, we were being ordered into Friedrichshouen in northern Denmark. That was difficult. The water was too shallow for our draught and we couldn't get in, so we set ourselves onto the anchorage and waited to see what they intended to do with us. We waited for two days, and then a fleet formation arrived from Kiel, a torpedo boat or corvette or frigate or whatever, one in front, one behind. They put us in the middle to keep an eye on us and escorted us into Kiel. We arrived there on Whit Sunday 1945, just about the last U-boat of the war to surrender'.

CPSIA information can be obtained at www.ICGtesting.com
Printed in the USA
LVOW021018011212

309622LV00006B/584/P